Making a Difference

Practice and planning in working with young people in community safety and crime prevention programmes

Compiled by

Alan Dearling and Alison Skinner

Russell House Publishing

First published in 2002 by:
Russell House Publishing Ltd
4 St George's House
Uplyme Road
Lyme Regis
Dorset DT7 3LS

Tel: 01297-443948
Fax: 01297-442722
e-mail: help@russellhouse.co.uk

British Library Cataloguing-in-Publication Data:
A catalogue record for this book is available from the British Library.

ISBN: 1-898924-39-2

Typeset by TW Typesetting, Plymouth, Devon

Printed by Antony Rowe, Chippenham

Russell House Publishing

Is a group of social work, probation, education and youth and
community work practitioners and academics working in
collaboration with a professional publishing team.
Our aim is to work closely with the field to produce innovative
and valuable materials to help managers, trainers, practitioners
and students.
We are keen to receive feedback on publications and new
ideas for future projects.

Contents

Acknowledgements   iv

About the authors   v

Preface   vi
Tim Newburn

Introduction: back to basics   1
Alan Dearling

Chapter 1 Community and neighbourhood strategies in work with
young people at risk   4
Alison Skinner

Chapter 2 Inter-agency action in youth crime intervention programmes   16
Alan Dearling

Chapter 3 Introduction to preventative work   21
John Pitts, Alan Dearling and Alison Skinner

Chapter 4 Staff development, programme planning and training   25
Alan Dearling

Chapter 5 Games and activities   48
Alan Dearling

Chapter 6 Befriending   57
Alan Dearling

Chapter 7 Working away from base   66
Alan Dearling

Chapter 8 Volunteers   77
Alan Dearling

Chapter 9 Working with the victims of young offenders: what works?   101
Brian Williams

Chapter 10 The school, youth crime and violent victimisation   114
John Pitts

Annexe: *from* Preventing school bullying   129
John Pitts and Philip Smith

Chapter 11 Working with violent men in institutions and the community   140
Alison Skinner and Gwyneth Boswell

Chapter 12 Mentoring socially excluded young people   149
Alison Skinner

Chapter 13 Participative evaluation   157
Jennie Fleming

Conclusions   168
Alan Dearling and Alison Skinner

Acknowledgements

The genesis of this book has been somewhat complex. Alan Dearling's involvement commenced as part of the team from the Vauxhall Centre for the Study of Crime at the University of Luton. Working particularly closely with Professor John Pitts and Alan Marlow, they helped to develop the Camden Youth Crime Prevention Programme. As a part of the process, Alan collated a 'compendium' containing a considerable amount of practice and programming material which had been previously published, but much of which is now out of print.

Alison Skinner joined Alan as co-editor of this book, and helped to provide a range of contributions with, and from, her colleagues at the Centre for Social Action at De Montfort University in Leicester.

The authors are also grateful for assistance received from specific individuals and agencies. In particular, they'd like to thank: Mike Thomas and the National Association for Youth Justice; Chris Taylor and NACRO; Howie Armstrong at NCH-Action for Children (Scotland); Trevor Locke; Philip Smith at Brunel University; Ann McDermott at Crime Concern; Julia Braggins at the Institute for the Study and Treatment of Delinquency; Peter Evans at the Home Office and Professor Tim Newburn at Goldsmith's College, University of London, who kindly agreed to write the Preface. Finally, a 'thanks' to Geoffrey Mann and the team at Russell House Publishing for helping to make this material available to the youth justice and related fields.

The book is dedicated to all the young people across the UK, from whom we've learned so much.

About the authors

Dr Gwyneth Boswell is Principal Lecturer in the Community and Criminal Justice Studies Unit at De Montfort University. A former Senior Probation Officer, she has spent the last eleven years as an academic, delivering pre-qualifying probation training and researching the backgrounds and custodial careers of violent young offenders.

Alan Dearling has been involved in some form of work with young people for about thirty years. This includes working in, and managing, the largest youth club in 1970s Europe, in Harlow; street work with punks and Rastafarians in London and the outskirts of Glasgow; and rural youth work and training in Dorset, East Lothian and the Borders. His special interest these days is work with Travellers and members of what had become known as the 'DiY' world counter-culture. He has been a research fellow at QUT, Brisbane, Cardiff, Brunel and Luton universities and is currently senoir research consultant for the Chartered Institute of Housing. He has writen and edited 24 books to date, many on youth work, including the near-legendary *New Youth Games Book* with Howie Armstrong.

Jennie Fleming is a Research Fellow and works for the Centre for Social Action at De Montfort University. She has worked in youth and community work for many years and in her current post has been involved in the participative evaluation of a large number of projects and written and published on the theory and practice of social action.

John Pitts is Vauxhall Professor of Socio-Legal Studies at the University of Luton. He has worked as a 'special needs' teacher, a street and club-based youth worker, a residential care worker in remand and assessment centres, a youth justice development officer in a London borough and a group worker in a Youth Offender Institution. His recent publicatins include: *Planning Safer Communities* and *Discipline or Solidarity: The New Politics of Youth Crime*.

Alison Skinner is an Information Officer and works for the Centre for Social Action at De Montfort University. Her subject specialisms include the youth justice system and work with young people at risk and she has written and edited publications in this field, including a Quality Framework for mentoring socially excluded people.

Philip Smith has worked as a probation officer and lecturer in social work. He is currently a research fellow at the Centre for Comparative Social Work Studies, Brunel University, where he has been involved in research into European child care and mental health systems.

Brian Williams is Reader in Criminal Justice and Director of the Community and Criminal Justice Studies Unit at De Montfort University in Leicester. His books include *Working with Victims of Crime, Counselling in Criminal Justice* and (as editor) *Reparation and Victim-Focused Social Work*.

Preface

Youth justice and community safety have undergone remarkable changes in recent years. New Labour came to power in 1997 promising to undertake 'root and branch' reform in these areas. To that promise at least, it was true. The Crime and Disorder Act 1998 saw the introduction of a new local statutory responsibility for community safety, and the creation of hundreds of crime and disorder partnerships. The Act also introduced youth offending teams and a broad range of new orders encouraging both earlier, and more intensive, intervention with young people. Further legislative change, the Youth Justice and Criminal Evidence Act 1999, has seen some of the principles of restorative justice extended to work with young offenders.

In this flux it would be all too easy to lose sight of the knowledge, the expertise and the experience built up by practitioners in the years prior to the reforms. As Alan Dearling says in his introduction, in these times where auditing, monitoring, performance management and league tables are increasingly coming to dominate practitioners' lives, how do we ensure that we continue to value and protect work whose qualities are not necessarily those being measured? This book is one important attempt to do just this.

What the authors have sought to do is to bring together a lot of practical information from disparate sources that will help inform and guide those currently working with young people in trouble. Moving from some familiar friends, topics like working with victims, and preventative work, to less familiar ones, such as befriending, and games and activities, *Making a Difference* provides a pragmatic set of ideas and tools, with instructive examples, that will benefit all those working in this field. The approaches don't always sit easily with much of what currently happens in youth justice and community safety work with young people, but that is one of the book's strengths. It asks, indeed challenges, the reader to think innovatively. In doing so, the contributors are ever careful not to overstate their case. There are no panaceas in this book. For good reason: there are no panaceas! This level-headedness is in stark contrast to that erratic journey from 'nothing works' to 'what works' and back again that we have been experiencing in recent years.

The title of this book, *Making a Difference*, is therefore well chosen. It recognises limitations: there are no simple solutions to the complex problems we face; there are no quick fixes. However, it is possible, as the contributors suggest, to 'make a difference'. Attempting to make that difference has to be done, as the compilers argue, with a clear view of the objectives that are sought, and of the principles and ethics that should guide action. Whatever your interest and concern in this field, men's violence, recruiting and managing volunteers, working with victims of crime, mentoring, practical ways of engaging young people, undertaking and managing practical evaluations, there are ideas, guidance, and examples in this book that will guide, encourage and provoke. At a time when it sometimes appears that novelty is all-important, it is vital that we should not lightly cast away the lessons of prior experience. *Making a Difference* is that reminder and I recommend it highly.

Professor Tim Newburn
Goldsmiths College, London
July 2001

Introduction: back to basics

Alan Dearling

The 'purpose' of this book is to provide practical ideas and information for those involved in direct work with young people – particularly those in trouble with the law or victimised by crime. Ultimately, at the centre of that work are young people, not abstract concepts of crime prevention, punishment or control, or even community safety. The only way to achieve the objective of diversion from crime is to focus on the young person. It is a matter of forging partnerships with them that seek to understand their needs, desires and the problems they face.

This book is essentially a compendium of tried and tested materials. It brings together practice-based methods of planning, preparation and running programmes for young people at various levels of intervention. These 'levels' themselves have been the focus of much heated debate over the years, and no doubt will continue to be so. Our collection is the product of many years' work undertaken by a diverse range of people working with young people in a variety of settings and agencies, stretching from the youth service, probation, social services, youth action groups, police, education, housing, health, the voluntary and non-governmental sector, community work and community development, through to tightly focused work done by youth offending teams, youth action groups and youth activity schemes dealing with offenders, and even prisons and young offender institutions.

In addition to describing methods of work, we hope that the book will help to provide a basis of principles and ethics for staff. Young people are expected to live and work in an extremely contradictory society. Therefore, managers and workers operating the whole gamut of community safety and crime prevention initiatives need to understand these contradictions as a part of the context which frames the lives of young people. Fundamentally, it is about determining the ground rules of engagement with young people – **what** we are doing and **why** we are doing it.

To start with, let's look at some of these contradictions:
- Young people are seen as (and indeed are) both perpetrators and victims of crime.
- They are expected to become citizens and stakeholders, yet are criticised for challenging authority and of failing to 'belong'. On the one hand they are encouraged to get involved, to take responsibility for their actions, and on the other, they find themselves without employment, forced on to low pay 'training schemes' and living with their parents into their twenties, still without a secure route into independence.
- They are urged to become 'included' rather than 'excluded', yet often cannot see where they 'belong'.
- They are frequently adjudged to be part of the problem, but social interventions need to work with young people to help them find their own solutions.

- Audits of crime and disorder need to be balanced with statements and targets of opportunities, such as for employment, adequate housing, access to education and learning, recreation, sport and leisure facilities and local transport.

The last few years of government and policy making in the UK has created a new environment for work with young people, especially those who are involved in offending behaviour and on the margins of society. Much of the focus has been on protecting victims and reparation, rather than broader social intervention to improve the lives of people in marginalised communities. Hopefully, managers and workers should not see these as mutually exclusive. And, in reality, it is the young people in many of the UK's most disadvantaged areas and communities who are amongst the most socially excluded. 'Youth' is a classic period of social marginality, but now, with severe structural unemployment in many areas of the UK, enforced training schemes, and lack of access to independent living, young people are denied or delayed from achieving adult status. This compounds the traditional adolescent problems encountered during the transition from youth to adult.

Meanwhile, the interventions from social work, education and the allied agencies are increasingly governed by audits, targets and the effectiveness of 'best value' programmes. Effectiveness is frequently measured in terms of protecting property, rather than in terms of people-empowerment. *Quality assurance* and *managerialism* have become fundamental components of the new orthodoxy. The Crime and Disorder Act 1998, is gradually providing the framework for much activity with young people. It is designed to protect and make safe communities, within a wider context of justice and control. In the guidelines for the training of the Community Safety Guidance Co-ordinating Group, it is argued that the implementation of the Act will put the *preventive process* at its core. This involves what it calls *anticipatory prevention* (Ekblom, 1998).

On the wider level, and usefully, Ekblom provides a model of *crime reduction* based on levels of intervention:
- Primary: *focusing on the general population of potential offenders, or of potential human and material targets of crime.*
- Secondary: *focusing on those at particular risk of offending or victimisation.*
- Tertiary: *focusing on those already convicted or victimised.*   (Ekblom, 1998)

This is the world in which the multi-agency partnerships and strategies will operate. The emphasis, while focused on victims and reparation, gives the key aim of the youth justice system as 'to prevent offending by children and young people'. Local authority departments, led from social services and education, in future have a duty to co-operate in providing an effective range of services under this banner of 'youth justice'. The 'youth offending teams' are the cornerstone of the implementation, with each youth offending team including at least one:
- social worker
- probation officer
- police officer
- nominee of the health authority
- nominee of the chief education officer
- plus other relevant nominees (for instance, registered social landlords, parish and community councils and NHS Trusts *must* co-operate, and many others such as the youth service, the courts and the drug action teams are invited to do so)

The reduction of crime and disorder has, therefore, become a shared responsibility for a great many local authority and related service providers. Underlying this strategy is the intention of making communities and their officers accountable for reducing crime through developing effective partnerships. To our mind, a vital element of this is to reassert the primacy of the basic principles by which managers and workers provide their contributions. Along with protecting property and victims, it is essential that those working with young people at any of the three levels, understand the needs of young people and can operate with them according to established principles, including:

- Ensuring the involvement and commitment of young people to any scheme (they are the most important partners, after all).
- An accord with human rights and the UN Convention on the Rights of the Child.
- Upholding the rights of young people to dignity, trust and self-respect.
- Empowerment, advocacy and self-determination.
- Confidentiality, which can at times conflict with accountability, rights and responsibilities.
- Access to adults who offer empathy, possess good listening skills and encourage young people to develop self-esteem and problem-solving approaches (in as creative a manner as possible).
- Opportunities for participation in non-stigmatising activities.
- Anti-discriminatory practice.
- Services which are holistic, that is, deal with the 'whole' young person, their personal, social and developmental needs and which help to support cultural and social diversity.

We hope that this book will do its bit to put this essential, child-centred, as opposed to problem-centred, essence back into the work undertaken by those involved in the new era of youth justice. If we forget that childhood and adolescence should be a period of excitement, challenge, adventure, mystery, magic and mistakes – we do so at our peril! And, we as managers and practitioners, must learn from our mistakes as well as our successes.

References

Ekblom, P. (1998) *The Crime and Disorder Act: Community Safety and the Reduction and Prevention of Crime*. Home Office.

CHAPTER 1

Community and neighbourhood strategies in work with young people at risk

Alison Skinner

Introduction

In many communities in the United Kingdom, including housing estates, villages, small towns and other types of neighbourhood, young people often find themselves the focus of attention and criticism from adults as they gather, in a highly visible way, on the streets of their home area. Action to engage with these young people is high on the current political agenda, via legislation and other programmes, but there is a danger of responses becoming over-punitive. Since levels of crime and lack of engagement in the economy have become the keys to unlocking access to provision and resources, the new challenge now centres on finding ways in which the legitimate demands of young people for a share in local resources and access to relevant services can be articulated and implemented.

This chapter will outline some of the ways in which young people usually come into conflict with their local community and look at some of the current models of intervention. The social action approach, as a way of enabling young people to articulate their own agenda, will be considered in detail.

Young people and residents: anatomy of conflict

Many young people are growing up in families affected by poverty and in areas with poor facilities and bad reputations, which are stigmatised by those living outside them. By the end of 1999, 26 per cent of the British population were living in poverty, measured in terms of low income and multiple deprivation of necessities (Gordon et al., 2000). Young people have no choice regarding their family circumstances, or where they grow up, but they have to deal with the consequences throughout their childhood and adolescence, which may include coping with lack of money, dangerous peers and adults, crime, prejudice from outsiders and unequal opportunities of education and employment.

There are wide-ranging social, family and individual circumstances which will influence the overall visibility of young people in their local communities. For example the lettings policies adopted by councils and housing associations can mean that many estates have a younger age-profile than the average. Other factors affecting whether young people are hanging around during the day or evening can include:

- Problems at school: a large self-report survey (O'Keeffe, 1994) found that nearly one in ten 15-year-olds truanted at least once a week and permanent exclusions reached 12,300 in 1998–99.
- Unemployment.
- Lack of legitimate money: many cannot regularly afford transport costs to visit shops or other towns, and leisure facilities may also seem too expensive for regular use.
- Perceptions of safety: many feel personally unsafe spending time away from their home area, or for the same reason are prevented by their families from doing so. This can affect both males and females.
- The reluctance of taxi drivers to travel to certain estates late at night.
- Lack of facilities in rural towns and villages.
- Cuts in the youth service both voluntary and statutory.

The consequences of all these factors are that large numbers of young people will often have little choice about how they spend their leisure time, other than being out and about in company with their friends, on their home estate or other areas during the day and the evening. Sometimes this can entail being exposed to personal danger and adult drug-dealing activities simply because they are out on the streets with no safe place to meet. More routinely however, their presence in significant numbers is likely to create anxiety among older residents, with subsequent calls to the police and the resulting possibly contentious police-young people contacts. Young people are residents too, however, and will usually express great loyalty to their home area, despite its shortcomings, since they feel supported by familiar surroundings and a network of friends and family. Although this may sometimes lead to 'turf' disputes with other young people on neighbouring estates, or villages, who have a similar strong sense of belonging to their own communities, there can be very positive benefits in this situation. As a task force to create change, young people have the assets of time and a very detailed practical knowledge of their local environment.

The conflicts that young people experience with other residents on their estates, villages and neighbourhoods can be many and varied. Some will be about the use of public space. Young people's legitimate desire to hang around together, use skates and skateboards and play football can simply not be accommodated in many cases without other residents feeling aggrieved and intimidated.

When young people are gathering on their local streets, this can also be about wanting to find some place where they feel safe, can exert some control over their surroundings, and find some focus for their interests and energies. This is experienced as a natural part of an age group growing up together in the same place. These needs are rarely articulated explicitly to anyone in authority, although the lack of such a place is likely to be a common complaint among the young people.

In finding a place to meet, it is often the case that where estates, villages or other areas have community centres, these may be geared more to the needs of young children or older community members. The activities that young people enjoy sometimes involve a degree of noise or disturbance that is unacceptable to older residents and teenage groups often end up being banned from these facilities after a few abortive tries. Purpose-built youth centres are not usually a standard feature on estates and the quality of youth provision available to young people can be very variable. If it is geared to the wrong age group, located in an unacceptable place, restrictive in the activities permitted, or promotes unacceptable messages, young people may either not use it or find themselves banned from it:

> The reasons given for the wholesale rejection of youth provision are the same as the reasons why group members do not use other community facilities such as the Sports Centre. They feel that the adult staff do not like them. 'All they ever do is tell you to stop smoking.'
>
> (Boulton and Smith, 1998)

Where young people find there is a mismatch between the organised facilities available to them and their fundamental needs, they will find their gathering places on the streets and in the nooks and crannies of their estate. A feeling of alienation from and hostility towards the adult community can then develop rapidly.

Coles, Rugg and England in their study of responses to young people on ten social housing estates note the following:

> Children and young people hanging around was common on almost all the estates in the study. However many of the professionals who were interviewed said that the biggest problem with hanging around was the responses of other residents who had forgotten what it was like to be young. Both the police and the housing officers reported high levels of complaint on this issue. They – together with the youth and community workers – often expressed the view that it has always been a common activity for children and young people to gather on the streets and that such action is not a crime.
>
> (Coles et al., 1998)

Faced with these circumstances, which are common up and down the country, residents' groups have two choices:
1. To try and control such manifestations by younger residents.
2. To acknowledge the legitimacy of young people's needs and work with them for change.

Many community groups initially try to control the symptoms of the problem rather than addressing its causes. In these cases, complaints to the police increase and they are regularly involved in action to move on and break up groups of young people on the streets, thereby jeopardising good relationships. Physical crime prevention measures may also be tried with better locks and bolts, alarms, linked fences, vandal proof paint and neighbourhood watch patrols.

Young people subject to these responses, which signify that the adult community is arming or protecting itself against them, will demonstrate extreme resentment of the position they are being forced to occupy and incidents of vandalism and crime are likely to be a constant undercurrent.

At this point, the community may well decide they need some outside help and a youth project, consultation, or initiative could result from this. The most important lesson to be drawn however, is that communities always have to engage with their young people sooner or later; the key question being when they do it and how entrenched attitudes on both sides have become before there is some intervention and mediation.

Currently there are a number of different models of intervention with young people in local neighbourhoods.

Models of neighbourhood intervention

The post-war period has seen a considerable amount of youth work and youth social work activity aimed at working with young people in their local communities. The rationale for this has varied with each decade, with detached work and intermediate treatment models operating in a broadly preventive role during the 1970s, until the focus switched to engaging with serious young offenders in the 1980s. The 1990s and the new century have seen attention turn back to neighbourhood crime prevention with the emphasis on targeted intervention.

The requirement for local authorities to develop strategies to address crime and disorderly conduct has led to a considerable amount of locally generated activity aiming to address different concerns. Some of these can be very narrowly focused however, with the main emphasis on stopping people doing things, rather than promoting community involvement.

Two major intervention programmes active in this field from a crime prevention perspective are *Communities that Care* and *Crime Concern. NACRO* and *Groundwork* have also been actively involved in this field.

Communities that care (CTC)

This has been adapted from an American programme and aims to create:
- A long-term programme for building safer neighbourhoods where children and young people are valued, respected, and encouraged to achieve their potential.
- A working partnership between local people, agencies and organisations to promote healthy personal and social development among young people, while reducing the risks of different problem behaviours.
- Up-to-date knowledge about the factors most likely to encourage self-efficacy, achievement and social commitment among young people.
- Local action plans whose principal goals are to:
  - support and strengthen families
  - promote school commitment and success
  - encourage responsible sexual behaviour
  - achieve a safer, more cohesive community.

CTC operates from a belief that there are influential risk factors in children's lives that increase the chances that they will develop health and behaviour problems as they grow older. These are identified as school failure, school-age pregnancy and sexually transmitted diseases, and becoming involved in drug abuse, violence and crime.

Their programme has a number of key elements:
- They create a working partnership between residents, organisations and agencies in the neighbourhood.
- A community-wide management board is formed, consisting of local professionals and community members who could include young people.
- A co-ordinator is appointed to liaise with the community and help the board create an action plan.
- An audit of the main risk and protective factors is conducted through a central consultancy provided by *Communities that Care* using a specialist auditing tool.

- The risk profile is used to select between two and five priority risks for action. This is followed by an audit of existing preventative services in the neighbourhood that are relevant to reducing those risks. The resources audit serves to pinpoint gaps in services and identify opportunities where existing work can be made more effective.

Programmes for young people are targeted at identified difficulties or deficits:

Community-based activities can complement the work of schools in helping young people understand the rights and responsibilities of citizenship. Specialist programmes can also offer support to young people whose early involvement in crime and drugs places them at risk of chronic difficulties by the time they reach young adulthood. Young people who leave school with few or no qualifications will be at heightened risk of unemployment and social exclusion without further education, training and work experience provided in the community.

(Utting, 1999)

As an intervention programme this scheme has a number of aspects which could limit its effectiveness in achieving its stated aims:

- The pre-set agenda requires communities to recognise that they are failing according to external crime-focused criteria, and to accept outside expert help, although they may be consulted and involved as much as possible.
- With the involvement of local professionals on the management board, it might be hard for community members to maintain parity of membership or criticise the performance of local services. Any young people participating are likely to be even more outnumbered by adults.
- There is a selective menu of approved intervention programmes that can be introduced to address specific problems – those recommended for young people include after-school clubs, mentoring, and employment preparation. These tend to reflect conventional views of what constitutes a successful intervention programme and promote a rather passive form of involvement on the part of young people. They do not allow young people to use their own initiative to find solutions to their own problems.

Crime concern

Crime Concern recommend a very similar framework in addressing community safety needs in a neighbourhood i.e. establishing an inter-agency group, carrying out a local crime and disorder audit, creating an action plan, targeting risk issues and working particularly on better estate security as well as enhanced community provision.

They do, however, place more overt emphasis than *Communities that Care* on consulting and involving young people:

Young people are the most frequent offenders and victims of crime. Local surveys show that young people hanging around in groups is the single most common cause of concern to adult residents on estates. Yet these young people are often doing very little wrong and the police can only move them on. When asked about their local needs, young people emphasise the lack of accessible and affordable leisure provision and their need for advice and help on a range of personal issues . . . Because they figure so prominently in crime issues, it is essential to consult and involve young people in any estate-based strategy. Reasons for this include:

– *young people know much more about local crime problems than most adults*
– *unless their own issues and concerns are taken on board, principally their high level of victimisation, young people will remain frustrated and disaffected by adult priorities*
– *young people have time, energy and commitment and can be a resource for getting things done.*   (*Crime Concern*, 1998)

Crime Concern recommend using a range of methods to consult young people including school-based surveys, informal group meetings, detached workers seeking the views of disaffected young people on the streets and establishing an on-going youth forum through which young people can make their views known to adults on the estate and to local agencies. They discuss ways of reaching young people who do not attend organised provision and programmes for young people most at risk.

While this model recognises the need to engage with young people in a meaningful way, developing a crime prevention or community safety strategy on the estate always has to be the starting point. Questions about their experiences of crime remain the chief conceptual filter through which young people's views are collected and passed on to the adults who have the real power to make changes in their neighbourhood. Young people are still in the role of passive recipients of youth provision, which is expected to help remedy some of their deficiencies.

Groundwork

This organisation has a broad-based remit to improve the social and physical environment in key areas that have been affected by economic decline. Working with young people is an integral part of *Groundwork*'s regeneration programmes. Projects to improve local environments and facilities provide young people with real opportunities to express their opinions, to develop their social and practical skills and to contribute to community well-being. Through this involvement, young people, often for the first time, feel they are not only part of the community but are also stakeholders within it.

A programme called *Youthworks* running from 1994-97 adopted a three year strategic approach to working with young people on five deprived housing areas in Blackburn, Hackney, Leeds, Plymouth and Sunderland.

At the local level a full-time project manager was employed to work with young people, as well as a network of full- and part-time staff and volunteers drawn from the local neighbourhood. A local development group that included residents, teachers, the police and the local authority supported them in their work. In addition there was a complementary youth development group with representatives on the adults' group.

Each *Youthworks* initiative started by carrying out an extensive audit of the estate to gain baseline information, gathering the views of adults, young people and local agencies. Its aim was to identify the key local issues and concerns which needed to be addressed and to establish a benchmark for monitoring and evaluation. Young people were involved in this exercise and groups of young people have taken part in a range of activities, including being involved in the development of play facilities on their estate. Criminal damage and vandalism were reported to have declined considerably (Grundy, 1998).

Although the estates chosen had significant crime levels the approach adopted offered a much more participative model for engaging with young people. There was a danger however in relying too heavily on the provision of activities at weekends and summer holidays and the relationship with youth workers. The community audit can become a one-off mechanism for establishing needs unless there is a recognised mechanism for regularly updating it. There is also a danger that the effects may wear off once the programme has finished and the workers leave. Creating a viable means whereby the community can carry on the initiative and continue to identify its own issues becomes important.

Social action

Social action is an alternative model for working with young people in their local neighbourhoods that starts from a different premise. It is a series of principles born out of the idea that change is possible. It is a theory of community development based on the premise that change can happen, but will only work if the people concerned own it and are involved in the changes they want. Its philosophy is summed up in the following six principles:

- Social action workers are committed to social justice. They strive to challenge inequality and oppression in relation to race, gender, sexuality, age, religion, class, culture, disability or any other form of social differentiation.
- They believe all people have skills, experience and understanding that they can draw on to tackle the problems they face. Social action workers understand that people are experts in their own lives and they use this as a starting point for their work.
- All people have rights, including the right to be heard, the right to define the issues facing them and the right to define themselves and not have negative labels imposed upon them.
- Injustice and oppression are complex issues rooted in social policy, the environment and the economy. Social action workers understand that people experience problems as individuals, but these difficulties can be translated into common concerns.
- They understand that people working collectively can be powerful. People who lack power and influence to challenge injustice and oppression as individuals can gain it through working with other people in a similar position.
- Social action workers are not leaders, but facilitators. Their job is to enable people to make decisions for themselves and to take ownership of whatever outcome ensues. Everybody's contribution to this process is equally valued and it is vital that their job is not accorded privilege.

Social action differs significantly in methods and approach from the other crime prevention methods of neighbourhood intervention described earlier, and from conventional forms of youth work:

- Residents or young people start with an open agenda to determine issues important to them, on the assumption that they are aware of key local concerns.
- Professionals are a resource to assist the group in achieving its goal, rather than taking a major role themselves.
- Young people and communities negotiate to achieve their own goals, learning a range of skills on the way.
- They follow a process of issue identification, analysis, action planning and reflection which allows change to develop organically.

- Residents and young people can be trained to take on the role of social action workers so there is less reliance on the stimulation of professional workers.
- Young people can think creatively about resources they can own and which take account of neighbourhood needs. Through their consumer views and perceptions they can assist local services to be more responsive to them and therefore more effective.

Social action and young people

The Centre for Social Action has considerable experience in working with young people on estates using social action methods and has published a handbook summarising the approach, including examples of work in practice and practical exercises (Centre for Social Action, 2000).

As a result of its experience of working with young people in many different areas, the Centre endorses the following beliefs:
- Young people are often marginalised and excluded from decision-making processes in their community.
- Despite this they are fully aware of the nature of the demanding and sometimes dangerous world they have inherited and are capable of working out for themselves the information, resources, advice and help they need to negotiate their transition to independence and adulthood.
- Their previous encounters with adult-run services have often been non-productive and inappropriate.
- Where they have been involved in decision-making their involvement has often been 'tokenistic' and has made them disillusioned and cynical.
- Young people have the time, talent, energy and potential to create their own resources in negotiation with the adult community.
- Their skills can be unlocked through a process of training, engagement and practice facilitated by an experienced worker.

Making contact: social action detached work

Social action workers often use a process of detached youth work to make contact with young people on estates and in their local areas. This ensures the involvement of larger numbers of young people living in the area, including those who do not wish to engage in the full social action process and those excluded from organised activity. Talking and listening to young people on their own ground is more productive than setting up a meeting in a venue where young people may not feel at ease.

There are several basic rules to social action detached work, most of which would be considered good practice in the detached youth work field.

Before meeting young people for the first time, all adults in the area need to be aware of the project and its purpose and the commissioning body, e.g. a housing trust, community group or voluntary organisation should provide suitable identification for the worker. Informing the police about the work is also a good idea. Social action researchers always work in pairs and, where possible, there should be a gender and race balance in the team. With the young people they should always be clear and open about who they are, the purpose of the work and how long they will be staying. The timetable for detached work in the first month must include daytime, early evening, later evening, weekday and weekend visits. If there is a school holiday, morning visits may also be necessary. If the area being researched is large enough, a grid system ensuring that all parts have been visited at all times can be used. Once a pattern of youth activity has been established, a map of this activity is drawn, showing which groups were encountered, where and when.

When the groups have been established, a suitable regular time for visits is negotiated. The researchers never ask the groups to be out on the streets at a time that suits their needs; the time arranged will be when the groups are normally out and when they are prepared to meet the workers. For this reason, during the winter months, this part of the process can take three times as long as in the summer.

The conversations with groups at this stage are structured into discussion areas: boundaries, use of resources, safety etc. The workers often leave the group with a question or something to think about for the next week. For example they may say: 'Next week we want to ask you about how safe it is to live here, where is less safe than here, what's the most dangerous place in the world to live?' They would ask the group to think about these things in the intervening week and provide a practical illustration of life on the estate. Pens and paper or perhaps a disposable camera would be left, so that the young people could make their own record. Since this work is done in groups chosen by the young people themselves, this dictates the age range and gender mix of the groups encountered during the detached work phase.

It is sometimes impossible to carry out the detached work in a meaningful way because of a lack of suitable meeting places on the street. If there are no lit areas on an estate, not even a phone box, then it is unlikely that a regular outdoor meeting of young people will take place. If there are no shops, no car park, no street lighting etc. then this phase of the work can prove difficult, when it entails working with young people in small groups of two or three at random times of the week. If there is no youth club or community centre open to young people on such an estate, then the social action researchers' task is even more difficult. They simply have to do what they can with the minimal opportunities available to them.

Working with the group

When the mapping work and the initial orientation phase is complete, the researchers usually end the detached work phase and begin the analytical and planning for action work with a group using an indoor facility. The groups may then sometimes be divided by age and gender.

The transition from the street to indoors is not difficult when a suitable venue exists. This should be a place where the young people feel comfortable: they should be asked for suggestions and involved in the booking of the venue.

An open invitation to all young people should be made and those who turn up for the first couple of weeks form the core group for the next phases of the work. At the end of these phases this group often takes on the responsibility for re-establishing contact with the young people who have chosen not to engage throughout the process.

The process in practice

What are the issues, concerns and problems that young people face?

The process can be started by asking the group what kinds of questions adults on the estate usually ask them? Typical responses are:

- *What do you want?*
- *What are you up to?*
- *What's the matter with you?*

This can be followed up by getting young people to talk about what it is like living on the estate, what they like and dislike about it, what makes them angry, what excites them and any other feelings they have about where they live.

This can be achieved through conversation with young people, but conversation is not necessarily the best means for all young people to express themselves. Those that are ready to talk often respond because this may be the first time in their lives an adult has asked questions and listened to them without feeling the need to argue, offer a different viewpoint, explain or criticise. Methods such as role play, drawing, music or games can be used.

Why do the problems and concerns exist?

This is a key question that distinguishes the social action process from many other types of neighbourhood intervention. Having helped the young people express what they see as key issues, they are then helped to analyse why these issues are a problem. Their judgement forms the basis of subsequent work: it will be necessary to ask questions to make sure they come up with a full analysis, but their views should be accepted, acknowledging that they will probably have a profoundly different interpretation of events than older community members.

In helping them take each of their issues and analyse the causes, the aim is to try to change the relationship between young people and adults. Their analysis needs to be treated seriously, but there is no reason why this need not be enjoyable for them: games, role-plays and other creative methods can be used.

Workers can ask questions about the key issues to help them think around the problem:
- *How long has it been like this?*
- *Does everyone agree with this thinking?*
- *Do you think it is the same everywhere or just on this estate?*

How can we change things?

At this stage the young people will need help in setting out their agenda for change. Once they have established what they want to alter they need to test out the best means to achieve their aims.

For example they might want to change the relationship between themselves and the police. Some may have strong feelings about this issue and will suggest methods that express their feelings, but don't help in achieving the aim. The workers' role in these circumstances would be to brainstorm all possible methods of responding to this issue, looking at the processes and consequences of the options and then enable the group to choose what method to adopt.

For change to be effective it must be decided upon and put into action by the appropriate community members: the young people. But this could be the first time the young people have tried to take power themselves. The task may seem daunting and failed attempts to decide on appropriate tactics may lead the group to become dispirited at this point. The workers' job at this stage is to keep up the momentum, and build members' confidence by breaking big problems into manageable tasks. They should not however do things to them, for them, or on their behalf. Young people must originate and control the ideas, analysis, planning and the next stage: action.

Workers should help young people assess whether the views expressed will help them achieve their aims:
- *Does anyone think that would be the best way to get what you want?*
- *Can anyone think of a different way?*

The young people can be helped to come to terms with what they want to do by taking it stage by stage:
- *How do you think we could start to do that?*
- *Who could we talk to at the beginning?*
- *Where could we get help to do that?*

Encourage them and keep them going.

Action

Workers will need to provide the means for the group to think through their agreed course of action, but ownership of the project should remain with the young people. Involving other people, particularly adults, may lead to a 'take-over' and this may need to be explained clearly to other parties.

The young people will need to be made aware of the constraints which may affect their plans, e.g. time, money and decision-making processes.

Workers could consider with them:
- *Have we thought of everything?*
- *Are we clear about our roles?*
- *Is everyone fully involved?*
- *Have we explained what is going on to everyone who needs to know?*

Reflection

Review the action by beginning the process again.

After each action has been taken, a forum for reflection needs to be created which allows young people to review what worked and what didn't work, why it didn't work and how it can be improved.

Sometimes the action taken results in a fundamental change that will allow the group to move on to other issues. Sometimes it alters the nature of the issue so that further action is needed.

Sustaining the work

The key to this kind of work is, wherever possible, to keep the cycle going and not make it a one-off event. Young people may often start with the need for a place to play football, or develop their own youth facility, and in one project the latter issue kept them engaged for over a year until they achieved their goal (Baldwin et al., 1982). In Bradford, where social action work was sustained in depth for five years up to the late 1990s, a group of young people developed a keen awareness of their health needs and initiated a critique of existing local health services. They worked with other agencies to see how these could be made more youth-friendly, in the course of the project articulating their own training and support needs, which were then facilitated by the social action worker they had interviewed and recruited themselves (Baker, 1999).

An offshoot of the social action process is that the ownership and momentum of the work provides a means whereby other problems can often be resolved. Young people involved in creative and productive change in their neighbourhoods come into conflict far less with other residents. If they then develop the self-confidence to question how their local community is policed, there is scope for productive dialogue with local officers that can create more positive relations and help lower crime levels. New skills and confidence can be translated into better performances at school when the relevance of learning becomes more apparent. A greater sense of personal fulfilment may reduce the need for drug taking to provide a distraction and a temporary sense of well being. The key point is that they are seen as having a right to organise and negotiate for their own resources without having to rely on the analysis and agendas of others.

Conclusions

Young people, their needs, activities and concerns are never very far away from public debate. A very considerable amount of effort and public resources are currently being directed to try and resolve many longstanding problems concerning their education, preparation for training and employment, health and behaviour. What is missing however is the scope for young people to act on their own initiative, learn skills for themselves and create change through their own efforts, negotiating on their own terms with the adult world. Social action is one method through which young people, currently viewed as problems in their local neighbourhoods, could become agents of positive social change.

References

Baker, S. (1999) Step 2 Project. *Social Action Today*. 10: May, 18–20.

Baldwin, J. (1982) *Give 'em a break*. National Youth Agency.

Boulton, I. and Smith, L. (1998) *Werrington Focus on Youth Final Report May 1998*. Centre for Social Action, De Montfort University.

Centre for Social Action (2000) *Youth Agenda: A Good Practice Guide to Working with Young People on their Home Ground*. Centre for Social Action and Guinness Trust Group.

Coles, B., Rugg, J. and England, J. (1998) *Working with Young People on Estates*. Chartered Institute of Housing for the Joseph Rowntree Foundation.

Crime Concern (1998) *Reducing Neighbourhood Crime: A Manual for Action*. Crime Concern.

Gordon, D. et al. (2000) *Poverty and Social Exclusion in Britain*. Joseph Rowntree Foundation, York Publishing Services.

Grundy, S. (1998) Old Problems, Young Solutions. *Social Action Today*. 7: Jan, 12–15.

O'Keeffe, D. (1994) *Truancy in English Secondary Schools*. HMSO.

Utting, D. (1999) *A Guide to Promising Approaches*. Communities that Care UK.

CHAPTER 2

Inter-agency action in youth crime intervention programmes

Alan Dearling

Why have inter-agency partnerships?

It is a much used (and sometimes abused) maxim in community-based work with vulnerable young people, that there should be a strategic, integrated approach to both the provision of services and support. Inter-agency working is intrinsically viewed as 'a good thing'. Cynics often refer to it as 'flavour of the month'. Proponents suggest that inter-agency initiatives provide 'best value' responses that add up to more than the contributions of the individual partners. None of this is new, although some of the language, rhetoric and focus of the work has changed over the last thirty years.

In 1993 *Crime Concern* published Jon Bright's influential book, *Youth Crime Prevention: A Framework for Local Action*. Within a framework of practical strategies for prevention of crime both by and against young people, the author identified the fact that many multi-agency partnerships underachieve because of a lack of clarity in roles, and probably because of a lack of ownership or stakeholding in the youth crime prevention strategies. His words of caution are worth repeating here as we consider how inter-agency work can be best implemented:

> *Multi-agency partnerships involve three sets of relationships which are not always thought through:*
> 1. *The relationship between agencies. There are many barriers to co-ordination between agencies and conflict frequently arises when agencies seek to work together in a sustained way for a period of time. These are not always easy to overcome.*
> 2. *The relationship between agencies and the public. It is important for multi-agency initiatives not to deskill communities and to ensure that all sections of the community are involved. Multi-agency initiatives should involve community representatives.*
> 3. *The relationship between agencies and particular crimes. There needs to be more precision about the role of different agencies at different points in the prevention of different crimes.*
> (Bright, 1993)

The absolute necessity for ensuring 'real' community involvement itself has a long history. For example, in a substantial report, *Developing an Integrated Approach, 1977–86* by the Canongate Youth Project (CYP) in the city centre of Edinburgh, the project authors focused on the community basis of their work as non-stigmatising or labelling:

> *Preventative work can be undertaken without accelerating young people into the welfare or legal system, community based services can be offered to a wide range of young people at*

different times, and when a local community are involved in this type of work they are much more likely to take on the responsibility for their troubled and troublesome young people.

(CYP, 1986)

Yet in their small group-work programme an average of 27 young people were worked with each year, with approximately 80 per cent being subject to some form of social work supervision order. However, the source of referrals came in 1986 from the social work department (55 per cent), the education department (30 per cent) and direct referral from families and the community (15 per cent). This range of referrals is probably more focused on an 'in need or at risk' group of young people than many of the more recent youth action and youth offending projects around the UK.

Indeed, it is very important that multi-agency initiatives look very carefully at **who** they are working with, as well as **what they are trying to achieve**.

At a governmental level, this targeting of, and prioritising of need, has been very evident in the first years of New Labour government. In particular, the 1998 Crime and Disorder Act and the 2001 National Strategy for Neighbourhood Renewal represent just two of the building blocks of 'joined up' thinking and strategic activity. Indeed the Neighbourhood Renewal Strategy's Policy Action Team (PAT 17) was called *Joining it up Locally*, while PAT 8 dealt with *Anti-social Behaviour* and PAT 12 with *Young People.* Out of this initiative, we now have £450 million in funds for the Children and Young People's Unit and the establishment of the position of the UK's first ever Minister for Young People.

Out of all this work, especially in the context of implementing the Crime and Disorder Act, any agency who works with young people in any way, or whose work has any implications on the lives of young people is now expected to contribute to inter-agency work. The earlier Youth Action Scheme investigated ways in which agencies working with young people could target and work with some of society's 'most at risk young people' (France and Wiles, 1996). They concluded that a 'strategy of different levels of intervention' is required to maximise the impact of the programme. This could be measured or monitored taking certain indicators into consideration (possibly types of reported crime involving weapons and violence; school incidence of occurrences involving weapons and violence; violence at youth service facilities).

Within any neighbourhood one can assume that there are a range of initiatives taking place, many of which may still be a direct response to the Audit Commission report *Misspent Youth: Young People and Crime* (1996) which recommended targeted responses for young people who seem likely to move from being involved in a delinquent act to becoming career criminals. These inter-agency initiatives require considering in terms of a process.

The inter-agency intervention process

Without trying to provide a definitive checklist for this process, anyone who is involved in creating an inter-agency youth crime initiative might wish to consider the following process model:

1. Define the potential range of strategies for prevention, intervention, diversion, and monitoring with regard to youth crime (or whatever).
2. Agree the aims and objectives of particular programmes. What outcomes or behaviour change is envisaged?
3. Establish an appropriate management and support system.

4. Identify resource implications: personnel, materials, agencies and organisations to be involved and timescale.
5. Seek funding, and inter-agency and community support and involvement in the scheme.
6. Engage in staff and worker induction and training as necessary.
7. Produce materials and resources as required.
8. Implement and monitor the programme.
9. Evaluate the effectiveness of the initiative.

Looking at precisely which agencies should or might be involved in any local area means thinking not just in terms of statutory agencies, but also voluntary agencies and members of the community. And in terms of the actual work with young people, if they are to be empowered towards new non-offending patterns of behaviour, then they must also be seen as 'partners' within the scope of the work.

The Home Office guidance on the statutory partnerships under the 1998 Crime and Disorder Act required:

> . . . the police and local authorities – together with police authorities – health authorities and probation committees, to work together, in partnership with other agencies to develop and implement a strategy for reducing crime and disorder.   (Home Office, 1998)

The other main partners are the local councils, registered social landlords and the NHS Trusts, with a long list of 'must be invited to co-operate' bodies also listed, ranging from schools and the youth service, through the fire service, to shopkeepers and trade union organisations: a real 'Uncle Tom Cobley and all' approach. The establishment of the youth offending teams under Section 39 of the Act required all local authorities, which had education and social work responsibilities to establish the YOTs, to actually co-ordinate the local youth justice services.

As is evident throughout the contributions in this book, the possible strategies for inter-agency intervention are varied in terms of their aims, and in their application and focus. As a universal theme, probably all schemes would hope to dissuade or prevent young people from what has become known generically as 'anti-social behaviour'. This term covers a multitude of greater and lesser criminal activity. At the 'serious' end of the spectrum this would mean involvement with weapons and violence, and then somewhere along the continuum of seriousness lie:

- racism
- persistent absence from school
- drug and alcohol abuse
- bullying and threatening behaviour
- theft
- vandalism
- vehicle-related crime

In terms of possible inter-agency responses it seems best to adopt a 'horses for courses' approach, which provides interventions appropriate for different community and institutional settings, and individual/groups of young people. Many of these are examined in more depth elsewhere in this publication, but the options for inter-agency work include potential interventions such as:

- intensive counselling
- individual treatment and behaviour change programmes

- reparation and mediation schemes, including victim support
- group work initiatives
- focused work programmes
- work with parents
- provision of new experiences and skills, including relationship building and self-esteem
- social action and outreach work
- employment programmes
- violence and weapons awareness programmes
- drugs and alcohol awareness
- personal health schemes
- anti-bullying and aggressive behaviour initiatives
- safe neighbourhood work

Moving towards good practice

If inter-agency work is to be effective and is to make a lasting and positive contribution in the lives of the young people in any given area, then it needs to move far beyond the work of committees. As agencies and their workers undertake an initial assessment (or audit) of resources and the scope of the programme, they must consider:
- Who is going to undertake the actual work?
- How much of the work is with targeted groups or individuals?
- How far can the work be community focused?
- How will referrals be made?
- How is the work going to be organised? i.e. what methods of implementation are going to be employed: counselling; presentations; interviews; videos; structured groupwork; be-friending; detached and outreach work; family work; residential trips etc.
- What types of evaluation are built in to the scheme?
- And, crucially, is funding available and adequate?

Wherever possible, the process of establishing funding requirements needs to involve the proposed staff team in the process. Consultation is fundamental to successful partnership working. Talking to parents and community members who live in areas where youth violence is common is part of the commonsense approach to tackling the problems 'on the ground', from **bottom up**, rather than **top down**.

Some of the indicators that can be identified where successful inter-agency interventions have taken place suggest that:
1. Young people need to be shown, in a way that affects them, the harm and suffering that the use of weapons and violence can cause to others.
2. They also need to recognise the implications that their actions have on their own lives and those of their parents and relatives, including their own potential incarceration.
3. More positively, young people need options for activities that are as exciting as violence, but contained in a legal setting.
4. Many young people only have a self-image that is negative; or one which is positive within a sub-cultural group (e.g. the gang). This needs to be changed.

5. Using and carrying weapons, and having a pre-disposition towards violence, is usually a result of the social situation. Gangs, racial conflict, parental absence and problems, lack of leisure, sport and creative opportunities all play a part.

One of the recommendations of the *Youth Action Scheme* evaluation (France and Wiles, 1996) was that the most effective work with young people on the margins of criminality is likely to employ primary and secondary methods of 'targeting' interventions at those already involved in 'unofficial crime, or minor or not persistent official crime'. This in turn represents a challenge to the ethos particularly of youth work and education services, where staff are used to working with all, or as many as possible, of their potential service users. Who should be referred to youth initiatives which are broadly of a crime prevention type is still a vexed question, as is, how to quantify the impact such schemes have. It continues to be a central concern of many inter-agency projects already undertaking this type of work.

For instance, in my own local area, Inspector Tim Warren in his first twelve month evaluation of the *Action Young People* scheme in Bridport, Dorset reports:

> The project started in September 1999, after agencies were invited by the Bridport police to assist them in identifying those people in Bridport in the 11–13 age group who were considered most at risk of becoming involved in persistent offending, serious drug or alcohol abuse or under-age pregnancy.   (Warren, 2001)

The scheme was unable to construct an accurate parallel 'control' group for their evaluation, but their report indicates that the inter-agency programme of mainly activities-based provision (i.e. community arts, a camping and outdoor pursuits trip, motorcycling, a weekly drop-in club) has had a quantifiable effect. According to questionnaire results from group members, parents, agencies and police, behaviour in the home, school and social life has improved for most members and their number of overall offences has, for the group of eleven young people, fallen from eleven in 1998–99 to five in 1999–2000.

References

Audit Commission (1996) *Misspent Youth: Young People and Crime.* Audit Commission.

Bright, J. (1993) *Youth Crime Prevention: A Framework for Local Action.* Crime Concern.

Canongate Youth Project (1986) *Developing an Integrated Approach.* CYP.

France, A. and Wiles, P. (1996) *The Youth Action Scheme.* DfEE.

Home Office (1998) *The Crime and Disorder Act, 1998.* Home Office.

Social Exclusion Unit (2001) *National Strategy for Neighbourhood Renewal: Policy Action Team Audit.* Social Exclusion Unit.

Social Exclusion Unit (2001) *A New Commitment to Neighbourhood Renewal.* Social Exclusion Unit.

Warren, T. (2001) *Evaluation of the First Twelve Months of Action Young People.* Dorset Police.

CHAPTER 3

Introduction to preventative work

John Pitts, Alan Dearling and Alison Skinner

In the late 1990s there was something of a renaissance of 'community prevention' approaches within community safety, youth justice and allied initiatives. Typical of this is the following statement by John Blackmore (Community Safety Officer, Brent):

> It is not sufficient to have a single high profile project which works successfully with a limited number of juvenile offenders. Such projects need to form part of a co-ordinated youth justice and youth crime prevention programme, actively led by local authorities in partnership with police, probation service, courts, health authority, voluntary sector and the community. If the private sector can be persuaded to demonstrate some sustained commitment then all the better.
> (Blackmore, 1997)

Relatively recently, Carol Martin co-ordinated the *ISTD Handbook of Community Programmes for Young and Juvenile Offenders* (first edition 1997). In the introduction to the book, Martin makes the point that the 1990s were dominated by the spectre of the out-of-control persistent young offender, following on from urban riots in towns as far apart as Newcastle, Luton, Oxford and Cardiff and the highly publicised Jamie Bulger murder. Given this context, it is perhaps ironic, that Martin goes on to describe the contents of the community programmes included in the book, saying:

> What became clear during the research is that the programmes which do target this rather euphemistically titled 'at risk' category are an extremely valuable community resource and need as much attention as any other type or group of programmes. (Martin, 1997)

Given that the ISTD survey of community programmes was the most extensive carried out in recent years, it is interesting to note that the common themes identified in the programmes, fall into four categories:
1. Victim awareness and empathy issues.
2. Management of anger and violent behaviour.
3. Drug and alcohol awareness.
4. Positive leisure pursuits.

Martin adds:

> . . . so many programmes are based on cognitive/behavioural skills and groupwork that they are not separately indexed. (1997)

During the 1990s and early 2000s, in a manner reminiscent of the original establishment of intermediate treatment, there have been various types of 'youth action groups' established under a range of initiatives linked to community safety. Those funded by the Department of Education and Employment were primarily aimed at promoting targeted youth work with young offenders by the youth service providers (France and Wiles, 1996). A number of these foundered because there remains resistance to what France and Wiles reported to be:

> . . . work (which) was seen to compromise the values and principles of youth work.
>
> (Adams, 1988)
>
> . . . similar arguments have underpinned youth workers' unwillingness to become involved with agencies such as the police (Markes and Smith, 1988).   (in France and Wiles, 1996)

France and Wiles concluded their evaluation of the scheme with the comment:

> . . . how little youth work has developed as a profession, compared with, say, teaching or social work . . . The professional development of youth work is important if the youth service is to play its role as an equal partner in multi-disciplinary and inter-agency responses to youth problems in general and crime in particular.   (1996)

An even more extensive scheme is the mainly school-based initiatives sponsored by the Prudential and *Crime Concern*, which seem to have led to wider scale developments, with:

> . . . 1,200 groups, involving the work of 20,000 young people in a quarter of all state secondary schools. The priority issues being tackled by these young people include bullying, vandalism, graffiti, personal safety, shop theft, bogus callers, burglary prevention schemes, school security measures and environmental improvements.   (Pru Youth Action, 1997)

A further shot in the arm for a back-to-prevention stance came from the Audit Commission's Report *Misspent Youth* (1996). That report recommended replacing ineffective court disposals with more preventative strategies designed to, 'guide young people towards constructive activities'. It is a close echo of Douglas Hurd's aim of offering 'attractive alternatives' with the establishment of *Crime Concern* in 1988. *Crime Concern's* briefing paper *Young People, Crime and Prevention* contends:

> In areas where there is a high level of offending by young people, it will usually not be sufficient to focus on just one aspect of a child's life or one stage of development. More broadly-based preventive action is necessary to ensure that there is continuity (over time), reinforcement (of standards in different locations) and inclusion (of young people in their communities).
>
> (Crime Concern, 1997)

Preventative work retains the attraction of being financially cheaper than custody, electronic tagging, or intensive supervision. It also increasingly includes elements of the restorative agenda, particularly 'proportionality', making appropriate responses that reflect the severity of offences. At the very least, it still offers social work, probation, housing, education, health authorities, the police and courts opportunities to work in ways which seem humane and caring, as well as containing a punitive element. This is just as possible in the youth justice system envisaged under the Crime and Disorder Act 1998, as it was in previous eras.

It is anticipated that the contents of this book will have some relevance to members of youth offending teams and youth offending panels, who are now being required to work with young people at risk and in trouble in new ways, following changes in legislation.

Since the advent of the Crime and Disorder Act 1998 the whole diversionary strategy regarding young offenders has been transformed, with new procedures introduced. The previous system of cautions has been abolished and Sections 65 and 66 of the Act has established the system of reprimands and final warnings. When a final warning is administered by a police officer they are required to refer children and young people to the local youth offending team for a 'rehabilitation programme' assessment.

If the assessment indicates the need for such a programme the YOT must produce one which:
1. Addresses the factors which contributed to the offending.
2. Describes the commitment the parent or primary carer can make in supporting the programme.
3. Describes the contact made or attempted with the victim.
4. Describes work planned to increase the offender's awareness of the harm caused by crime, or to make reparation.   (Youth Justice Board for England and Wales, 1999)

In addition to intervention at this stage there is also a new point on the tariff for first time offenders. Part 1 of the Youth Justice and Criminal Evidence Act 1999 provides for a Referral Order, which is intended to become the standard sentence imposed by the youth court or other magistrates court for children and young people convicted of an offence or offences for the first time. These will normally be referred by the court to a youth offender panel who will establish a programme of behaviour which the young person will be obliged to observe. The principal aim of the programme will be the prevention of re-offending by the child (S.8(1)). Section 8 identifies typical components of a programme of intervention which include:
- Financial or other forms of reparation to the victim of the offence.
- Mediation sessions with the victim.
- Unpaid work as a service to the community.
- Conditions that require the child to be at home at specified times and attend school or work.
- Specified activities to 'address offending behaviour' or to serve rehabilitative purposes with respect to drug or alcohol misuse.
- Reporting conditions to persons or places.
- Prohibition from association with specified persons or places.
- Compliance with the supervision and recording requirements of the programme.

The terms of such a programme will form the basis of the 'youth offender contract' (S.8 (6)) which the young person will be required to sign. Once the programme of behaviour has been established and the contract signed, the progress of the young person will be subject to review by the youth offending panel (Goldson, 1999).

The implementation of the Act is still in its early stages and it is not yet clear how YOTs and youth offending panels will interpret their responsibilities. There are concerns in the field about the philosophy, assumptions and procedures underpinning this diversionary approach, well expressed by Goldson (1999) and Haines (1999). Modifications may well take place as the new systems bed in, but in the meantime staff need to think about the type of programme which might best deliver these objectives.

Haines sets out some principles regarding work with young people that should apply to the operation of youth offending panels:
- *The best interests of the child should be the defining principle of the aims of panels, in full recognition that in so doing measures to promote the prevention of re-offending will be maximised.*

- *Representation on panels should include agencies and organisations who have general and specific responsibilities to protect and provide services to children. Panels should be managed in such a way to ensure these agencies' responsibilities are properly discharged.*
- *The measures applied to young persons under the youth offender contract should reflect the age and maturity of the young person, their degree of culpability and the seriousness of the offence.*
- *Particularly for young and minor offenders, overly intrusive measures which focus on criminogenic need are inappropriate and should be replaced by interventions which seek to promote positive behaviour.* (Haines, 1999)

References

Adams, R. (1988) Finding a Way, in Jeffs, T. and Smith, M. (Eds.) *Welfare and Youth Work Practice.* Macmillan.

Audit Commission (1996) *Misspent Youth, Young People and Crime.* Audit Commission.

Blackmore, J. (1997) Community Support for Young People. *Criminal Justice Matters.* 28.

Crime Concern (1997) *Young People, Crime and Prevention.* (Briefing paper 4) Crime Concern.

France, A. and Wiles, P. (1996) *The Youth Action Scheme: A Report of the National Evaluation.* DfEE.

Goldson, B. (1999) Wither Diversion? Interventionism and the New Youth Justice, in Goldson, B. (Ed.) *The New Youth Justice.* Russell House Publishing.

Haines, K. (1999) Referral Orders and Youth Offender Panels: Restorative Approaches and the New Youth Justice. in Goldson, B. (Ed.) *The New Youth Justice.* Russell House Publishing.

Martin, C. (1997) *The ISTD Handbook of Community Programmes for Young and Juvenile Offenders.* ISTD/Waterside.

Pru Youth Action (1997) *Partners for Life: Young People and Community Safety.* Crime Concern/Pru Youth Action.

CHAPTER 4

Staff development, programme planning and training

Alan Dearling

Introduction

Staff development and training can be viewed on at least two levels:
- The first is as a range of responses, structures and processes which enable staff to learn skills, gain experience and receive appropriate support and supervision. Essentially, it is about **how staff learn and can be supported**.
- The second relates to the specific competences that relate to working with young people across the spectrum of crime prevention. This is primarily about **what they need to know and the appropriate skills**.

Taking the latter topic first; the range of tasks which may be undertaken by people as responses to youth crime is enormous. Throughout this book we have presented examples of initiatives which represent parts of this response mosaic. And one significant element in that mosaic is the much vaunted multi-agency partnership, discussed earlier in Chapter 2, *Inter-Agency Action in Youth Crime Intervention Programmes*. It is the very fact that work in the arenas of community safety, crime prevention and crime reduction blurs into many professional, community and even academic domains, that makes discussion of 'core training' and 'competences' so difficult. The professions involved in management and training for disciplines such as probation, social work, police, housing, education (including youth and community work) and health have a hard time delineating their own professional curriculum.

Ownership and stakeholding in community safety varies through different localities in the UK and among the different service professions. Many probably feel that they'd like to get more involved in strategic and practical responses to youth crime, but it is likely to be the implementation of the 1998 Crime and Disorder Act that forces them to do so. That Act was very wide ranging in its scope, and unusually, was introduced by the Secretaries of State for the Home Department (Home Office) and for Environment, Transport and the Regions, plus senior representatives of the Local Government Association and the police. Community involvement was stressed in the introduction and is mentioned throughout, as are the many layers of 'partnerships' that are needed to make safer communities a reality. However, in terms of guidance on statutory partnerships in training there do seem to be some internal contradictions present between the overall aims of the Guidance, which states:

> *Training strategies will need to underpin the legislative aims to break down boundaries between criminal justice organisations and others concerned directly and indirectly with crime prevention, crime reduction and community safety.* (Home Office, 1998)

and the more specific guidance from Paul Ekblom (1998), which stresses the need for 'the development of a professional discipline'.

This more detailed Guidance appears to focus on the training and education needs of the core professional groups involved: the police, probation and members of the criminal justice system, with social services, architects, health, housing, education and related service providers being seen as outside the 'dedicated expert practitioner' grouping.

In this section, we offer some alternative models of what training, competences and staff support mechanisms may be required. We still view volunteers (and paid part-time staff) as an important component of staff teams, so make no apology for including a specific section on them a little later in this book.

The following is an extract from *Community Safety and the Reduction and Prevention of Crime: A Conceptual Framework for Training and the Development of a Professional Discipline.*

As the main Guidance on training shows, the range of competences required of practitioners in the crime prevention field, reduction and community safety is extremely wide. But the central defining features of professional practice in this area must be a thorough working knowledge of:
- The causes of criminal and disorderly events, risk and protective factors.
- The offender's perspective on crime opportunities – risk of punishment, effort and reward.
- Evidence-based interventions, and how these work in particular contexts.
- Implementation both directly and through 'action at a distance', and the perspective of these front-line preventers themselves.

In identifying the core competences for prevention, experience suggests that a 'cookbook' approach, rigidly applying preventive methods drawn from a limited repertoire, is inadequate. The ability to apply theoretically sound principles through a practical, problem-oriented approach is vital. This approach has become known simply as the **preventive process** (a term which has close affiliations with Problem-Oriented Policing). It is the tactical equivalent of the strategic process set out in the Guidance on Audits, and involves several stages:
- Homing in on specific crime and disorder problems identified and targeted through the strategic Audit and target-setting process, by collecting and analysing more detailed local information.
- Local target setting.
- Devising preventive action closely tailored to the specific circumstances, with interventions based on evidence of effectiveness or through application of sound principles.
- Monitoring, evaluating the action and its impact on the local and strategic crime targets, tuning and reviewing.

Promoting community safety involves developing competences to:
- Understand the hierarchy of human needs that are threatened by crime and disorder, and be aware of people's potential to tackle those hazards themselves or cope with the consequences.

- Attempt to hold each of the hazards below the tolerable levels on a sustainable basis and without undue adverse side effects on other aspects of social and economic life, such as privacy, liberty and aesthetically-pleasant environments, and without promoting inequity or exclusion.
- Empower the public individually and collectively to contribute in acceptable ways to socialisation of the young, informal social control of (convicted and potential) offenders and self-protection from crime and disorder.
- Help people cope with the crime and disorder they do experience, and to remedy the suffering, costs, restrictions and fear which their perceptions and experience of these engender.
- Bring people's perceived risk of crime more closely in line with objective risk (taking account of both the likelihood of the hazards and the severity of their consequences).

(Ekblom, 1998)

Skills for working with young people

This book is essentially about working effectively with **young** people. To our mind, some of the core skills required by such workers involve them developing the ability to:

- Encourage young people to take responsibility for their own actions, to develop social and practical skills, to respect other people's rights, and develop their own self-worth in an empowering fashion.
- Effectively provide challenges for young people, within a sensitive and caring environment, which enable them to develop coping strategies and alternatives to offending behaviour.
- Offer empathy and good listening skills.
- Help young people to develop good relationships with their peers and adults.
- Work as a member of a team.
- Make assessments of young people's attitudes, behaviour and cognitive abilities, which involve the young people themselves in developing personal action plans.
- Provide information about rights, responsibilities and available resources.
- Develop a toolkit of skills and techniques including groupwork, counselling, advocacy, social action and individual treatment programmes.
- Understand and partake in programmes involving reparation, mediation, peer-tutoring, victim support and other justice and reconciliation techniques.
- Develop an anti-discriminatory framework.
- Work appropriately on sensitive and personal development areas such as: gender; race and ethnicity; religion; sexuality; drugs and health.
- Liaise and co-operate effectively with other agencies and workers.
- Set targets for their own work and take part in evaluation.

Somewhere in this list, there should also reside the necessity for staff in this field of work to have a good knowledge and understanding of themselves (strengths and weaknesses), to be self-critical and to have a measure of self-esteem and assertiveness. A sense of humour helps, too!

Additionally, it seems appropriate to be reminded of what was said at the end of *Worth the Risk* in relation to some of the basic aims of juvenile justice work:

We feel that empowerment of young people within juvenile justice, is no less important than either systems management, or wider political lobbying for reform of penal practice.

Some of us might subscribe to the view that for young offenders, 'it's a fair cop but society is to blame'; but one way of ensuring the powerless stay powerless, is to ignore their basic rights: the right to be heard, the right to be respected (if not for their actions, at least for themselves), the right to take risks, the right to express feelings and opinions, the right to expect legitimate help, the right to believe in themselves, and the right to personal dignity.

(Ball et al., 1987)

Determining aims

One of the greatest dangers inherent in the work is that good intentions do not in themselves make a good worker, nor do they in any way guarantee that the interventions will be effective. To train workers, trainers and organisations need to have clear (and achievable) aims and goals for their work. As Mike Anderson said:

Too often, however, there is just the hope that something positive will happen if a 'good', 'appropriate', or 'meaningful' relationship can be built with children by 'caring' adults.

(Anderson, in Locke, 1981)

Mike went on to describe two broad categories of aims:
  1. Delinquency related.
  2. Personal growth.

It may, therefore, be possible for agencies to determine training and staff development needs in relation to the aims and more focused goals of their intervention programme. For instance, if the focus is on reparation and victim/offender mediation, staff skills and responsibilities are obviously different than for a programme focused on diverting a group of young people on a housing estate from vandalism and anti-social or threatening behaviour. And, while different, both schemes may require staff to possess advocacy skills, as they act as a 'buffer' between child and victim, child and parents, child and authorities.

Lucy Ball and Theo Sowa covered some of the same territory in their *Groupwork and I.T.* (1985). Their example of programme aims included:
  1. To stop offending.
  2. To contain young offenders.
  3. To provide alternatives to custody.
  4. To change offending patterns.
  5. To develop self awareness about offending etc.

Elements of staff planning for group work and other programmes.

To achieve the aims and objectives in any youth programme, the importance of motivated, appropriate staff members cannot be over-stressed. Ball and Sowa's book focused on group work, but their commentary about 'Leadership' and 'Values Clarification' is still important for anyone charged with looking at staffing issues in youth justice (or similar) programmes. Here's what they suggest.

Leadership

Leadership will be strongly influenced by the expectations and behaviour of group members, some of which you can change or influence and some of which will be out of your control. You therefore need to be aware of what is happening within the group and to remain sensitive to its needs. The way you lead the group may need adapting as group dynamics change. Remember that as groups develop they go through various stages. The groupwork jargon for this is 'forming, storming, norming, performing'. Although we sometimes joke about these terms, they have often been helpful in facilitating our understanding of group dynamics. We have found that groups usually will take time to get to know each other, will then test boundaries and having established those boundaries will function more effectively. The group as a whole may be influenced by issues or events which could affect their attitudes or behaviour in a workshop. For example, if a group member has just been given a custodial sentence you may need to deal with that issue rather than carry on with the planned workshop.

A group will probably not always feel like 'a group'. At any time, but especially at the beginning, there may be potential problems such as age differences, animosities which exist outside the group, racism etc. which split the group. You will need to handle these issues sensitively and to choose suitable methods to deal with them. Some examples of ways of dealing with group issues are:

1. A large group meeting where the issue is confronted head on.
2. Preparing workshops which will directly deal with the issue.
3. Preparing a workshop or activity that indirectly encourages greater understanding or friendliness.
4. Dealing with the group members individually etc.

Having fun as a group always helps group dynamics! It is good for group leaders and group members alike to have informal times together. This can happen within sessions or by organising specific activities such as cooking and eating meals together. At the Junction Project we also have a 'residential' away for two nights during the programme. They are exhausting but we have usually found them to be an effective way of promoting group cohesion.

Boundaries

Before the group starts you need to decide what your boundaries for it are going to be and how you are going to keep them. The boundaries established are likely to vary according to the type of group you are running, e.g. compulsory or voluntary attendance. Some boundaries will inevitably not be negotiable e.g. no physical abuse, but you may want the group to be involved in making some of the boundaries e.g. how long will you wait for latecomers. If it has been established that group members are to be involved in the setting of boundaries, it is essential to allow this to happen. Do not pretend to give this power to the group. If you do have a structure where the group can influence some boundaries it may be helpful to decide on a specific time in the week or day where these discussions can take place. It is of paramount importance that it is clear to you and to the group what the limits of 'acceptable' behaviour are. We have also found two further guidelines useful in keeping boundaries. Firstly, what logical and rational reasons there are for them. Secondly, that the reasons are explained to the group so that they understand fully the need for those boundaries.

Everyone needs to know what will happen if set boundaries are crossed. There may be different sanctions for transgressing different boundaries and for the extent of the transgression. We have found that some of the most effective sanctions are those negotiated by the group. It may be useful to have a warning system which operates before sanctions are invoked. If boundaries are crossed, do not ignore the situation. It is tempting to not quite see or hear what you would prefer not to deal with. However, situations that you fail to deal with rarely go away. They usually make it more difficult to sort out those you do choose to deal with. The other danger is that if you wait too long to act, a situation which may have been improved may become irretrievable.

If you are co-working or part of a larger team it is important to keep the same boundaries and respond in the same way when they are crossed. There are few things more undermining of other workers than reacting differently or not reacting at all to agreed procedures on control issues.

You need to decide what your boundaries are in your relationships with the group and individual group members. What is the role that you are going to adopt within the group? There are various options, for example 'friend', 'boundary keeper' (emotional or physical), 'rule enforcer', 'protector', 'observer', 'advocate', 'carer', 'teacher' etc. We have found that there is often conflict for workers between the roles of 'friend' and 'boundary keeper'. Workers are naturally keen for group members to like them, but this can lead to difficulties if this can not be balanced with the responsibilities workers carry for keeping the group within agreed boundaries.

You may adopt more than one role or different roles at different times. The nature of your participation in the group will be influenced by the role you decide to adopt, for example the extent to which you actively join in group activities or sit back and watch.

The issue of confidentiality is one of the most important boundaries' to establish when running groups on offending. A group needs to know what will be shared with their families, project workers, social workers, the police etc. They also need to know how freely they can talk about past (or present) crimes without repercussions. Group leaders should clarify these boundaries well in advance of the group (values clarification) and ensure that they are agreed with the group as soon as possible.

Co-leading

These materials could be used by a single worker running a group work programme. However, in this section we concentrate on issues to do with co-leading. We will be referring to two workers, although it is possible to co-lead with more. When we refer to 'co-leading' we mean that workers endeavour to share the responsibility of planning and running the group. There are various reasons why you might want to co-lead, for example to share skills, to build up confidence, to initiate new techniques. Some of the benefits of working in such a way are that it:

1. Can bring more skills to a workshop.
2. Can be a more supportive structure both for the workers and the group.
3. Gives scope for developing the workshop by allowing workers to take on different roles so that they can look after the different needs of the group e.g. group dynamics and materials development.

Some of the difficulties of co-leading are that:

1. Differences between workers could be manipulated by the group.
2. Workers could undermine each other.
3. It can involve more work, for example in sorting out differences in values amongst workers, in co-ordinating with each other, in watching out for your co-worker as well as group members in workshops etc.

Co-leading and planning

Before you start working with the group, it is important to sort out your differences in attitudes and make sure you have established some ground rules for yourselves. Set up your structures for communication, for example, when you are going to meet to prepare workshops and to discuss how the programme is going etc. Both workers should be involved in the planning of the workshops, from shaping the overall programme to dealing with the minutiae for example who is going to introduce the workshop, present different materials, draw out comments from the group members etc.

After the workshop, look at how it went. Be honest about the issues that arose, whether they were positive or negative. It is important to deal with mistakes as this will improve the practice of both workers. Regularly check how supportive you are both being and make plans to avoid awkward situations which may have arisen. If you do not say what you want you will not get it!

Co-leading and roles

Make sure you have sorted out the roles that the group leaders are going to have in a workshop. There are different ways of dividing up the roles e.g. on the basis of who is more confident in an area, on the needs of the group, on areas workers want to develop skills in etc. We have found it useful to have one worker concentrating on the group task and the other concentrating on the group dynamics. This can be helpful, for example in situations where certain members of the group are not participating. The worker dealing with the dynamics can ensure that those members of the group are drawn into the workshop, while the other worker carries on with the task. Another example is when you are dealing with either a very difficult or energetic group, when one worker can deal with any control issues that arise, while the other completes the task, ensuring that some of the aims have been achieved by the end of the workshop. Remember that roles do not always have to stay the same. In particular where you are dealing with control issues, it is important to swap the discipline role so that one worker does not get labelled 'weak' and the other 'hard'. Finally, during the workshop do not undermine your co-worker by taking over their agreed role.

Values clarification

The importance of **values clarification** in group work with young offenders lies in the extent to which hidden or unclear values can affect a group work (or any other) programme which spends considerable time exploring notions of 'right' and wrong 'good' and 'bad', both in legal and moral terms.

This is not to say that workers should approach workshops 'objectively'. We do not believe it is possible or necessarily desirable to be value-free. The importance lies in workers being clear about their values so that personal values do not distort practice to the extent that aims and objectives become unattainable.

Values

It is important to explore the kinds of values held by the workers before they start working on values-related issues with groups. For example:
1. What are your attitudes towards the police?
2. What are your attitudes and beliefs about young offenders?
3. Do you feel differently about different types of offences?
4. What are your positions on issues of race, sex and class?

Values can be reflected in terms of the overall format of the programme. For example:
1. Who are the group members?
2. Why is the group being held?
3. Why have you focused on certain topics within the programme?
4. To what extent is the programme an attempt at 'socialisation' or moving the group closer to an accepted norm?
5. To what extent should it be such an attempt?

Values are also reflected in the dual workshops which are actually run:
1. What kinds of questions should the group consider?
2. Why?
3. To what extent did your personal values dictate which materials, methods, topics etc. are used in the group?
4. How do your values affect the ground rules and boundaries agreed within the group, e.g. confidentiality, decision-making etc.

Hidden or unexplored values can lead to confusion through mixed messages, unconscious manipulation of materials and group dynamics, and alienation of some (or all) members of the group.

Co-working

Values clarification is also extremely important when co-working a group. Workers will always have some differences in their values and approaches. If these are clear, they can be worked on, which allows a potential for improved co-working. (It also means that it might be more difficult for group members to manipulate the workers.) As long as the workers can reach agreement on some basic 'rules' (e.g. decision-making, programme content, use of authority etc.) and feel comfortable with their differences, then these differences in approach and values can be beneficial to the group. However, if for example, one worker belongs to the Socialist Workers' Party and the other to the Monday Club, it is not difficult to imagine how their personal values could prevent their being able to co-work effectively in workshops dealing with issues such as policing, court systems, police image etc. It is possible, and sometimes necessary to sort out differences between co-workers within the group. As long as this is dealt with constructively, this could be good for the group.

Training and values clarification

At the Junction Project we have found that staff training has been important in helping us to clarify our values and to use that knowledge to improve our practice. For example, concerning issues of race, staff members have attended racism awareness programmes individually and we have invited external trainers to work with us as a team on issues of racism within intermediate Treatment as a whole and our project specifically. As a team we have also explored our attitudes towards working with offenders who have committed crimes that we find hard to deal with (e.g. rape). Other issues have been equally important e.g. our attitudes towards custody, our attitudes towards and beliefs about the youngsters who attend the project (young, male, working class, black and white).

Although our training in these areas is very important we have found that the training is necessarily only a beginning or a catalyst. The hard work comes afterwards in relating what we have learnt, to the way in which we plan our programmes and work with youngsters.

Various games manuals contain some very good exercises which can be used for values clarification. For example, *Groupwork Practice* (Douglas, 1981) *Gamesters' Handbook* (Brandes and Phillips, 1977) and Dearling and Armstrong's *New Youth Games Book* (1994).

In this section, we are not advocating that workers come to definite, earth-shattering conclusions about their values. However, we would argue strongly that workers allow themselves time to take a good, hard look at their values and become more aware of how they affect their practice; this has to be a continuous process. Remember that clarifying your values is not an end in itself: its usefulness lies in using that knowledge to improve your practice.

Providing appropriate training

Over the years there have been innumerable training courses run for staff involved in some aspect of work with young offenders and community safety. Considerations for making choices, both as managers and participants, include:

- who runs them
- who they are for (and any entry or experiential requirements)
- levels of planning
- course content
- length and aim of courses
- qualification or personal development
- involvement of 'learners' in course content
- relevance to job requirement

The TNA process consists of four main stages:

1. The identification of training needs.
2. Deciding about which needs should have priority.
3. Providing the appropriate training.
4. Evaluating the success of training provided.

The process is often represented in the form of a loop, as shown in the accompanying diagram. The concept is a very simple one. Any organisation which wishes to undertake a genuine TNA must start by identifying its training needs and then prioritise them in the form of a training plan. Once these steps have been completed, the training can be provided, probably by a range of diverse learning methods. It is then essential to evaluate whether the training provided has met the organisation's needs. The process of evaluation may well throw up additional training needs and so the process continues. The loop is often termed the 'Training Cycle'.

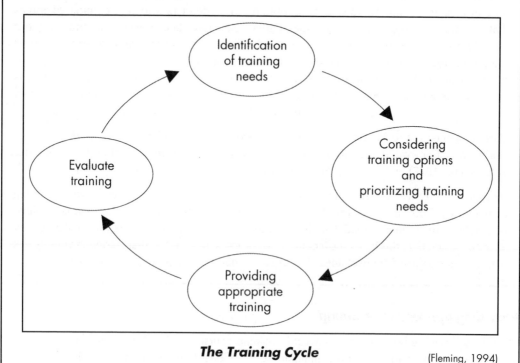

The Training Cycle

(Fleming, 1994)

All of these may be relevant indicators of 'appropriateness'. At a personal level we may want to re-train as an aromatherapist, but this might not be the most **appropriate** training need for us, either to tackle the job in hand, or to meet the skill requirements of our organisation. In an ideal situation, both the training needs of the individual and the organisation's team need to be prioritised and then balanced. But, as with any balancing act it can get tricky.

One important tool for helping to ensure that the organisation and staff receive the most appropriate training, is called Training Needs Analysis (TNA). Below is a brief description of this process from *Training Needs Analysis for the Leisure Industry*.

As a framework for how to evaluate these needs, managers must look at:
1. Organisational training needs.
2. Job analysis.
3. Individual needs.

1. Organisational training needs

These are the strategic and development needs of the organisation. For instance, it may be that the plan is to move into intensive group work, and away from individual, offence-focused work. Or, maybe the agency wants to focus on school-based work. In either case this might require refocusing training needs in a particular way. The advent of mission statements, business plans, quality assurance, audits and organisational performance indicators should always be linked to a re-evaluation of training needs. Unfortunately, training and staff support is often overlooked. This can seriously undermine staff competence levels, staff potential and ultimately the overall performance of an organisation. John Pitts, in Chapter 10 of this book, *The School, Youth Crime and Violent Victimisation* highlights the need for the culture of the institution (in that case, the school and teachers) to be seen as the key to behaviour and attitude change. Casson and George (1995) say, '. . . the culture of an organisation is far from a mere detail, and is arguably the most fundamental of all policies'.

As the aims and goals of an organisation change, so do the training needs, and the culture of the organisation needs to adjust to accommodate this process. There may be external as well as internal factors at work. Have a look at the following examples and then consider drawing up your own training needs checklist for your organisation.

External factors (to the specific agency or team):
- legislative changes
- administrative or IT changes
- new partnerships
- new directives
- changed emphasis on styles of working
- new government priorities
- demographic changes
- changes in offending patterns
- changes in court referrals

Internal factors:
- management style and leadership
- new staff members or managers

- budget changes
- staff leave
- policy changes
- changes in the location of work
- changes in the focus of client group

2. Job analysis

Earlier in this section we have already looked at some of the likely skill areas required by staff working with young people. Skills and tasks are related to the overall aims of the agency and purpose of the particular job. In terms of achieving these aims it is important that organisations relate the job descriptions they use to help identify areas of training need. A job description usually covers:
- pay and conditions
- accountability structure
- organisational aims
- purpose of the job
- detailed functions of the job
- experience or qualification required
- location of work, hours and special requirements

You might consider using these checklists to identify whether staff are indeed skilled to do the current job on hand, or whether any mis-match can help to identify training needs. This might be as simple as needing a female member of staff to co-lead a mixed group, the need for a qualified driver to develop off-site work, or the introduction of complicated new referral procedures.

Without becoming too oppressive, the measurement of the effectiveness of a staff team or an individual might be developed into a set of procedures which measure performance against criteria. These could include looking at the range of expected interventions and the intended outcomes, and processes such as good recording and evaluation of inter-agency liaison, and methods of individual contact work with young people. This theme will be returned to a little later.

3. Individual needs

Tony Morrison, in *Staff Supervision in Social Care* (1993) used the term 'staff care' to describe a holistic type of programme for developing staff support and supervision systems. His focus was on 'supervision', but the models are equally for trainers/supervisors and learners/supervisees. At the individual level, Tony identified ways in which individuals could develop their own 'self-care' plans, in co-operation with peers and managers. Training and support needs might easily be integrated into this model. To our mind, Tony rightly identified stress as one of the main problems faced by social care staff. Here is a self-care plan and list of affirmation and action points adapted from Morrison:

Individuals engaged in stressful types of work, need, and should expect to receive:
- Adequate support and supervision, ideally, both at professional and personal levels.
- Ample opportunities to discuss and reflect on their work, both as an individual and as a staff team member.

- Access to knowledge and training to develop their skills and aptitudes, and to understand the aims and tasks involved in different components of their job.
- Opportunities for personal and professional advancement.

A self-care plan for managers, supervisors and supervisees

1. Clarify what your roles and responsibilities may or may not be. Role confusion is a primary cause of stress.
2. Analyse the use of your time, clarify your priorities and think of strategies to regain more control over your time.
3. Read about the nature and management of stress. Information is empowering.
4. Decide whether your current ways of dealing with problems are helpful and how they could be improved, particularly in terms of how you do or don't ask for help.
5. Think of ways in which you could get more out of supervision and training by:
   - Being clearer about its purpose and mutual expectations via a contract or a renegotiated contract.
   - Ensuring that regular two-way feedback is part of the process.
   - Checking out any fears or fantasies you have.
   - Naming and working through 'stuck' processes in supervision and training.
6. Set realistic expectations for yourself and those around you. Are you in the right job? Are you meeting the right needs through supervision and training? Do you accept that you cannot change some people and situations? Give yourself permission to learn from mistakes.
7. Ensure you have an active leisure life which includes regular exercise and relaxation. Maintain a high level of self-awareness.
8. Learn to be more assertive and reduce both unwanted compliance and aggression.
9. Stay focused on the issue or task when dealing with problems. Avoid personalising things.
10. Accept that you cannot anticipate all stress.

Affirmation and action points

1. What skills, knowledge, values or attitudes in your current practice can you affirm?
2. What skills, knowledge, values or attitudes do you need to change or develop?
3. What help do you need from other people to make these changes?
4. What training needs arise from this?
5. What policy needs arise from this?
6. Consider one specific, achievable change you wish to make.

Support, development and appraisal

Some of the greatest dangers inherent in building a system to facilitate staff support are that they can become mechanistic, meaningless and judgmental. Where systems of performance appraisal and performance review work well, they are likely to be only a part of a genuinely empowering and participative structure of staff care. They offer the opportunity to review previous performance, plan constructively and positively for future work, identify strengths and weaknesses, training needs *and* organisational and individual changes which could improve performance and effectiveness. Sadly, this sort of process can easily degenerate. Then it becomes a chore both for manager and staff member. It can also become the source of future conflict, especially where the process and its outcomes result in sanctions, including pay restraints.

Underlying some of the problems in this process are accountability and power. Many staff are attracted into working with young people with problems because they feel that may be able to help them, empower them even. Such staff may well feel that their main accountability is to the young people. This can be in stark contrast with organisational or management aims, which may be to curb offending behaviour, or organise reparation for victims.

Professional development

This section ends with useful material based on two publications with which Tim Pickles was involved. The first is *Social Care Professional Development Systems* (Watts, Pickles and Miller, 1993). In that book, three of the main sections feature material designed to help social welfare teams:
- identify professional development needs
- plan to meet those needs
- manage a professional development system

Throughout their book, the authors tried to strike a balance between the agency's needs for their staffs' personal professional development and the individual's personal and career motivations. Their model for developing professional development systems starts from using an *Individual checklist*, which needs to be tailored both to the agency and the team members, with a good deal of care and foresight.

In the section on managing the system, they suggest that it is important for managers to consider a number of related issues. These could include the following (in relation to staff development plans):
- What budget amount is reasonable and appropriate for each member of staff?
- How many days per year might this translate into?
- What balance is struck between individual and agency needs?
- Where should professional development sessions take place?
- How many sessions should occur as a whole agency, team or specific to the individual?

There are a number of ways to arrive at a personal checklist of needs that can then be prioritised in order to develop an agreed programme for personal development. Watts et al. (1993) suggest five:

1. Responding to immediate workplace demands
For example, 'I must look that up', or 'I must ask so-and-so about this'. But it is very hit or miss, and unlikely to provide priorities for identifying and pursuing needs.

2. Diary studies
By keeping a brief recording of work undertaken, a member of staff may be able to identify skills and competences, and areas of weakness and need.

3. Peer counselling (or tutoring)
This requires a level of trust and mutual understanding of the other person's work. The process usually involves one person describing one or two problem areas in their work. The listener then can offer prompts to elicit more information about the scenario and lead on to an analysis of knowledge and skills which would help the individual to tackle the problems confronted. This may form the basis for identifying needs. It is very dependent upon the skills and knowledge of the 'listener'.

4. Critical incident analysis
This formalises and extends the previous two techniques. On a sheet of paper, a particular event is described, where the individual feels that they made mistakes or could have handled the situation better. They then make a list of skills and knowledge deficits, and finally, prioritise that list.

5. Checklists
These can be developed by an individual, team or agency to identify the most important skills, competences and knowledge required to tackle jobs in the workplace. The process can assist in prioritising development needs at each level, and can be as specific or general as required. For instance, health and safety requirements might be mentioned, the need for assertiveness, or very specific skills needed for working with a particular client or customer. When deriving a checklist in this context, it may be possible to create headings, each of which requires its own list. Watts et al. (1993) suggest:
- *management of self*
- *management of others*
- *levels of work*
- *knowledge base*

as useful checklists.

Checklists and any other identification of personal, team or agency development needs can then be further prioritised and may become part of the information integrated into performance appraisals. These form part of the evaluation process which should be built into any training and staff development systems.

Performance management

Performance appraisal, as already intimated, is a many-headed hydra. It can be many things to many people. Hope and Pickles (1995) in *Performance Appraisal* suggest that it is most beneficial to agencies and their staff when it is part of a 'performance management'. This is their diagram explaining:

Rather obviously, performance appraisal systems can be used for reward, punishment or development. Usually they are a mixture of the three. They also need to be integrated with other management and training systems. Where performance appraisal is part of the formal system, it is likely that at the 'heart' of the appraisal system there is a formal meeting, which takes place once or twice a year, based on a process defined by the use of appraisal forms. The procedure for such a meeting will vary between organisations, but it may involve:
- The use of pre-meeting checklist forms for use by the appraiser and the job holder.
- A formal meeting at which the pre-meeting forms are exchanged.

Where, when and how appraisal takes place

FORMAL	
Appraisal happens in planned meetings on an individual or group basis. It may be called: • supervision • performance appraisal • staff review • critical incident analysis.	Appraisal happens in unplanned discussions on an individual or group basis where the assessment or feedback is agreed at the time—usually as the result of an unforeseen crisis or problem but away from the point of service delivery.
PLANNED	**AD-HOC**
Agreement in advance is reached between individuals or members of a group to give feedback and constructive criticism whilst doing their work. Appraisal is a continuous process of assessment and feedback to a person or a team. It may be recorded and reviewed regularly.	Appraisal is tacitly given while individuals are working. People give and receive feedback, criticism, advice, etc. It happens often but is unplanned. It arises as circumstances allow.
INFORMAL	

• Production of a summary appraisal form which is signed by both parties.
• Production of a professional and personal development and training needs or plans.

The sample forms from Hope and Pickles at the end of this chapter help to explain the aims and the process. They are pretty typical of the forms we have seen used both in social welfare agencies and in commercial organisations.

Performance appraisal is likely to be most effective in organisations where:
• It is part of an on-going process.
• It is separated out from considerations of pay, discipline and promotion.
• Non-hierarchical appraisal takes place along with that by line managers.
• It leads to personal development and training opportunities which are valued by staff and management.
• There is genuine stakeholding in the system from staff and management appraisal system.
• Everybody understands how the system operates.
• Confidentiality is respected.

Hopefully, this will provide you with enough material to consider some of the pros and cons of appraisal systems. The Hope and Pickles' book, *Performance Appraisal* (1995) provides a much more in-depth description of the systems and outcomes.

A brief conclusion

Without good planning and staff support, training and supervision, effective work with young people is seriously impaired. The necessary 'trick of the trade' is to balance the need for flexibility and responsiveness in work with young people together with the needs of staff for adequate and appropriate development opportunities.

Sadly, in reality, the skill and attitudes base for much work in youth justice often receives short shrift. Similarly, elements of spontaneity and risk-taking, which are so much a part of youthful behaviour, can easily be overlooked when youth crime initiatives are designed and implemented. However, as we try to show throughout this book, an understanding of young people and their needs, causative factors in crime, and a realistic appraisal of staff needs are all key facets in planning successful preventive interventions with young people.

References

Anderson, M. in *The Aims of IT Groups*, Locke, T. (1981).

Ball, K. et al. (1987) *Worth the Risk? Creative Groupwork with Young Offenders*. SCF and West Yorkshire Probation Service.

Ball, L. and Sowa, T. (1985) *Groupwork and IT*. London Intermediate Treatment Association.

Brandes, D. and Phillips, H. (1977) *Gamesters' Handbook*. Hutchinson.

Casson, S. and George, C. (1995) *Culture Change for Total Quality*. Pitman.

Dearling, A. and Armstrong, H. (1994) *New Youth Games Book*. Russell House Publishing.

Douglas, T. (1981) *Groupwork Practice*. Tavistock.

Ekblom, P. (1998) *Community Safety and the Reduction and Prevention of Crime: A Conceptual Framework for Training and Development of a Professional Discipline*. Home Office.

Fleming, I. (1994) *Training Needs Analysis for the Leisure Industry*. Longman.

Hope, P. and Pickles, T. (1995) *Performance Appraisal*. Russell House Publishing.

Morrison, T. (1993) *Staff Supervision in Social Care*. Longman.

Watts, P., Pickles, T. and Miller, A. (1993) *Social Care Professional Development Systems*. Longman.

Annexe 1 Pre-meeting job holder's checklist (Hope and Pickles, 1995)

This checklist is to help you plan your appraisal meeting with your appraiser. Fill in the form and use the checklist as an agenda for the meeting. You may need to refer to other papers such as your job description and the work programme to fill in this checklist and during the meeting.

This checklist is confidential to you and your appraiser. It may also be seen by a third party if needed.

Your name:

Job title:

Location and date of the appraisal meeting:

Your job

1. What is the overall purpose of your job and what are your main job responsibilities?

2. What is it about your job that you:
   (a) Like?   (b) Dislike?

3. What style or way of working do you prefer?

4. In what ways has your job changed since the last appraisal session?

5. What changes in your job would you like to make?

Your skills

6. What are the main skills you need to do your job?

7. In carrying out your job what additional skills or knowledge would you find useful?

8. What skills or knowledge do you have that are not used in your present job but you would wish to apply in the organisation?

Your performance

9. What aspects of your performance are you pleased about and want to continue?

10. What aspects of your performance are you disappointed with and want to improve?

The organisation's performance

11. What aspects of the way the organisation works have helped or hindered you in your job (systems, procedures, culture, etc.)?

12. What aspects of your line manager's performance are you pleased about and want to see continued?

13. What aspects of your line manager's performance are you disappointed with and want to see improved?

Annexe 2 Pre-meeting appraiser's checklist (Hope and Pickles, 1995)

This checklist is to help you plan your appraisal meeting with the job holder. Fill in the form and use the checklist as an agenda for the meeting. You may need to refer to other papers such as your job holder's job description and the work programme to fill in this checklist and during the meeting.

This checklist is confidential to you and the job holder. It may also be seen by a third party if needed.

Your name:

Job title:

Location and date of the appraisal meeting:

The job holder's job

1. What is the overall purpose of your job and what are the main job responsibilities?

2. What is it about the job that you think the job holder:
   (a) Likes?   (b) Dislikes?

3. What style or way of working do you think the job holder prefers?

4. In what ways has the job holder's job changed since the last appraisal session?

5. What changes in the job would you expect the job holder to want?

The job holder's skills

6. What are the main skills the job holder needs to do the job?

7. In carrying out the job what additional skills or knowledge would the job holder find useful?

8. What skills or knowledge do you think the job holder has that are not used in the present job but could be applied in the organisation?

The job holder's performance

9. What aspects of performance are you pleased about and want to continue?

10. What aspects of performance are you disappointed with and want to improve?

The organisation's performance

11. What aspects of the way the organisation works have helped or hindered the job holder in the job (systems, procedures, culture, etc.)?

12. What aspects of your performance in regard to the job holder are you pleased about and want to see continued?

13. What aspects of your performance are you disappointed with and want to see improved?

*Annexe 3 **Appraisal summary sheet*** (Hope and Pickles, 1995)

Appraiser's summary of the session

Job holder's summary of the session

Appraiser's signature   Date

Job holder's signature   Date

Third party involvement

If agreement cannot be reached a third party can be asked to facilitate a further meeting to assist you to find a way forward. Please indicate whether this is required.

Confirmation of appraisal process outcomes

Job holder's line manager (or appraiser's line manager if appropriate) review of completed form.

Signature   Date

When completed this form should be copied to the job holder, the appraiser and the line manager within 10 days and be kept confidential.

Annexe 4 *Career and personal development plan* (Hope and Pickles, 1995)

Name:

Job Title:

Date:

Training/development needs
(Skills, knowledge, awareness etc.)

Possible ways of meeting those needs
(Job development, special projects, coaching, training, job shadowing, etc.)

Action plan
Who will do what and by when?

-

-

-

-

-

Skills inventory
Skills or knowledge you have that are not used in your present job but could be of use to others in the organisation?

Copies of this form should be kept by the job holder, the appraiser, the line manager and the personnel officer.

CHAPTER 5

Games and activities

Alan Dearling

Introduction

The use of games and activities has formed the cornerstone of programmes of work with young people since the nineteenth century beginnings of youth work, which in its day was mainly conceived as a 'child saving' movement. Two centuries ago, the 'heavy end' of the justice system was not on the street, or in the community, but in the prisons, which were seen as 'reformatories' for young delinquents. Anthony Platt said of the child savers in America:

> . . . (they) were not indulgent sentimentalists; they recommended imprisonment as a means of removing delinquents from corrupting influences.   (Platt, 1969)

But in Britain, if not in the United States of America, 'recreation' and 'social activities' were seen as being an important part of philanthropic youth work, even as early as 1878. Maude Stanley, an early pioneer of 'rough boys' clubs', said that social activities were:

> . . . pleasures which helped much to educate them in other ways than book learning, making them feel that they were cared for by those above them in position . . .
> (quoted in Booton, 1985)

The context in which games and activities can be used effectively

The reason for mentioning this very early history here, is to remind users of this book that the swings in favour, for and against the use of games and activities in preventative and intervention programmes with young people, is neither new nor novel. By the 1980s, there was a considerable backlash against the use of so-called recreational methods in the work with young people in the criminal justice system. It was seen by some as 'treats' for offenders, and there was some truth in the argument that intermediate treatment and youth social work evolved at the expense of mainstream provision for young people in many areas of the UK.

Now, in the age of crime prevention and community safety schemes, there has been a cautious move back towards once again utilising games and activities within both general community-based schemes in areas of high juvenile offending, and as part of a more tightly focused youth justice schemes. Within general youth work provision, which is, after all, part of primary crime prevention provision, their use has never gone away. For those working either with 'high risk' young people or those already convicted, workers have often found that they have to do more than concentrate entirely on the individual, offending behaviour and measures of reparation and atonement. So, for pragmatic reasons, 'social education' as it was once known, has evolved into a 'youth work curriculum' which mirrors the stages of intervention better known to youth justice workers. Recent research at the University of York, on working with young people on housing estates, broke the elements of youth work down into four component parts:

Components of youth work

Diversionary activity
This can be defined as leisure and recreation-based activity such as sports, crafts, and discos. Its aim is principally to present interesting things for children and young people to do.

Developmental work
This work carries a more profound purpose than simple entertainment. Rather, it aims to use different activities to develop self esteem and confidence amongst children and young people. A diversionary project would be to run a youth football team, whereas a developmental project would be to help children and young people to run a football team.

Centre-based work
This is any work with children and young people based at a specific locality, for example, a school annexe, a purpose-built youth club, a community centre or sports facility. Centres are likely to provide a focus for both diversionary and developmental work.

Detached youth work
Detached youth workers go into the community and talk with children and young people where they naturally congregate, for example, cafes, bus shelters or street corners. This work is often aimed at groups that may include members with problematic relationships with schools or their families. The purpose of the engagement can vary, but (in the context of this report), most of the detached work had the purpose of getting these children and young people involved in diversionary, developmental and centre-based work.   (Coles et al., 1998)

Broadly, this model describes the general settings in which activities and games might be used by adults working with young people. In the model, structured youth justice groups would be seen as part of 'developmental work'. However, for many workers who meet young people as a consequence of a court appearance and referral from a youth crime panel or youth offending panel, the developmental work is more clearly focused on what the Home Office has called, 'crime prevention interventions' (Ekblom, 1998).

Why use games and activities?

Much has been written about the use of games and activities in work with young people including by myself and Howie Armstrong (1994; 1995; 1996). See also Jelfs (1982); Priestley and McGuire (1983); Ball et al. (1987); Brandes (1977 and 1982); Dynes (1990); Institute of Social Inventions (1990); and Paget (1990). Some of these publications focus on work with offenders and young people at risk of offending or causing nuisance, others are more general books on games and activities. Additionally, there is also a considerable body of knowledge about using the outdoor environment as a resource for creative activities with young people, both in general youth work programmes, but also in specific programmes for those perceived to be at risk of offending or known to the youth justice system, see for instance, Cornell (1987); Maclellan (no date); Smith (1994); Dearling with Armstrong (1997), and Cooper (1998). These and other resources we have included in the references at the end of the chapter, since there is no intention to replicate these publications here, nor would it be possible to do so, for reasons of space.

Within the context of community safety and crime prevention work with young people, some of the reasons for using games and arts and crafts are more specific than in general 'play', 'recreation', 'sport', 'arts', 'leisure' and 'youth work', but taking the **general reasons** first, they provide opportunities for:

- having fun
- excitement, stimulation and creativity
- social and physical interaction
- improving co-ordination and communication skills
- developing a new hobby, sport or leisure pursuit
- building confidence and social and other skills

In specific developmental youth work settings, such as group work with young offenders, games and activities may be purposely chosen and adapted to help young people:

- develop trust, sensitivity and awareness
- improve their relationship building skills with both adults and other young people
- improve their literacy and numeracy
- identify personal (and group) problems and develop strategies to overcome them
- consider drug and alcohol abuse, sexuality and relationship issues
- take responsibility for, and become accountable for, their actions
- cope with aggression, stress, loss and other difficult to deal with situations
- consider the effects of their own behaviour on others and help them change their behaviour
- look at, and inter-act with, the built and natural environment and their local community
- carefully consider very specific incidents of offending behaviour

Importantly, games and activities give the adult workers new opportunities to build relationships with young people. From this base, it is possible for staff to develop more appropriate and effective work in other ways such as reparation, mediation, mentoring, cognitive behavioural and restorative justice programmes.

What sort of activities and games are useful in prevention and diversion?

The following games and activities are all ones that have been used in social groupwork programmes with young people. They are adaptable and can be used in a variety of settings, including in fact, staff development training. Because they are often passed on by word of mouth, it is difficult to give an exact source of many of the activities, but I have given a reference to the place where I first discovered the particular activity.

Planning is a vital part of using games and activities, as is the need for staff to feel confident that they understand what an activity entails, its potential pitfalls and the need for sensitivity and possible debriefing at the end of a session. In my experience, it is also useful to consider a mix of activities which are 'lighter' and 'heavier' in their content and purpose. Often the opening game or activity is referred to as an 'icebreaker' or 'warm-up' game, whilst more personal sequences are known as 'relationship games'. Other games are sometimes classified as 'trust', 'contact', 'co-operative' or 'group task' games. Using a combination of these and possibly some arts and crafts or outdoor activities allows the young people (and the adults) to feel less threatened and encourages participation. Finally, it is important that workers see activities as something they are willing to participate fully in themselves. At times this may make staff feel uneasy or vulnerable, but if adults expect young people to take risks and be honest, then they must do the same.

Height, age and name

This works well at the very beginning of a new group. Ask everyone to organise themselves in a line by height, ending up with the tallest person at the front. When they've done this successfully ask everyone to give themselves a clap. The sequence ensures that everyone will make physical contact and will have moved around the room a bit. Then, ask them to organise themselves by age. This means that they all have to talk to one another. Again, when it is completed, ask everyone to say their age in order, which helps break the ice and gets people used to talking in front of the group. A further variation is to ask the group to sort themselves in order of the alphabet by first names, so Adam would come before Alan, who would be in front of Anne. The trick is to make sure that these sequences are completed fast.

Shoes

I first met up with this ice-breaker when it was used by Philip Hope, who is now an MP. In a largish group, tell everyone to take off their shoes and put them in the middle of the room. Then, the facilitator quickly scrabbles all the shoes up, stands back and tells everyone to put their shoes back on as quickly as possible. The result is usually something of a physical riot, so best not done in the room next to the Principal Social Worker!

Seriousness of offences

This is based on a sequence described by Priestley and McGuire (1985). The idea is that members of a group are given a list of about twenty offences. Alternatively you can write them up on a flip-chart. Then ask each person individually to rank them in order of seriousness with the most serious at the top of the list. Another option is to get each person to choose the four most serious, and the four least serious, offences.

I've also run this sequence using votes. Everyone has five or ten points which they can award in any way they wish to what they view as the most serious offences. After the voting, it provides the basis for a discussion on similarities and differences in the way the offences have been ranked, and on whether crimes against property or people are seen to be the most important. Some examples, in no particular order:

- setting fire to a building
- driving over the speed limit
- stealing sweets from a shop
- burglary of a TV and video from a house
- stealing a car
- driving without any insurance
- being arrested for drunkenness
- rape
- maiming a cat
- breaking a shop window
- taking £5 from your mother's purse
- beating someone up
- carrying an air rifle without a cover on it
- exposing yourself in a public place
- stealing CDs from a shop

Situation cards

This is one of the most adaptable methods of promoting discussions between group members on topics which may be 'difficult' or 'confronting'. Howard Armstrong and myself described this in our very first *Youth Games Book* compendium back in 1980 (current edition 1994). You have to plan this one in advance, making up a set of cards which are appropriate to the ages and experiences of group members. We've also made up sets for staff training to enable workers to think about potential problems and situations that they may face for real. With a group of young people who have been involved in a range of delinquent or nuisance behaviour, cards could include:

> What would you do if a mate had taken some crack cocaine and was experiencing serious problems?
> A friend offers you a mobile phone which you know is stolen.
> A fourteen-year-old girl who you know well tells you she thinks she is pregnant.
> A friend tells you he has beaten up another person earlier in the day and wants you to provide an alibi if the police catch him.
> A policeman seems to always be picking on you.

To run the sequence usually requires preparing about 20 cards. Then the group facilitator invites people in turn to take a card, read it aloud, and then to give their response to the situation as though it is actually happening to them there and then. The facilitator should then encourage everyone in the group to express their views on the particular situation. There is no one answer to any situation but there may well be legal points which are worth raising as well as possible moral ones.

Ideally, allow enough time so that everyone has had at least one go at dealing with a situation.

Meeting the police

This is based on the programme developed by the Save the Children Hilltop Project (Ball, 1987). Often young people only see the police as negative authority figures, and their contact with them only occurs when there has been an incident of some kind. Inviting a police officer, a magistrate or some other adult, possibly even an ex-prisoner, can be an opportunity for young people to challenge their own prejudices and also to meet an adult figure on neutral territory. At the time of writing this book, I'm involved in a local youth video project in Dorset and our youth team invited the local community policeman, Nigel, along with the mayor, arts workers etc., to our planning meeting. He was regarded as just another adult, albeit in a uniform!

Likewise, Hilltop suggest involving police and other adult authority figures in ways which avoid being confrontational. They ran a pre-meeting brainstorm session with the young people during which a range of possible questions are suggested. After getting them written up on a flip chart, the questions are written onto individual cards and each group member asks one or more question during the meeting. Hilltop stress that it, '. . . ensures that the questions asked are the ones which members want to ask, and provides anonymity for whoever wrote the questions.' They add, '. . . it is important to prepare the speaker for the session by explaining what is expected.'

Does crime pay?

This is a discussion session devised by Lucy Ball and Theo Sowa (1985). The aim is to get group members to consider what they have gained and lost through offending. The facilitator needs a flip-chart and a felt pen.

The first stage is to 'brainstorm' by asking everyone in the group to quickly call out the good things that they've gained from offending. This might include 'money', 'having fun', 'excitement' etc. Then repeat the process with the bad things that have happened to them as a consequence of offending, perhaps sentences, a criminal record, rejection by their family etc.

Finally, the facilitator leads a discussion on the two lists, including options for getting the 'good' things legally!

Personal shields

There are various versions of this activity. This is again based on the Hilltop collection. A facilitator draws a shield on a piece of paper or card and photocopies it for each group member. The exercise provides an opportunity for self disclosure and for thinking about future aims and goals. Each shield is divided into sections, which allows the person filling it in to identify aspects of their own behaviour, strengths and weaknesses (see next page):
- Things I'm good at.
- What I'd like to become.
- My good qualities.
- Bad points about myself.
- How I see myself in a year from now.
- Motto (a phrase or saying which sums up my attitude to life, for instance, *live for today*, or *death or glory*).
- Epitaph (an inscription about me which might be written on my tombstone).

Who am I?

This is known by various names. It's an arts activity for non-artists and is a visual version of Personal Shields. In preparation, the facilitator needs to have obtained a largish role of redundant wallpaper or printers' paper, some water-based paints and some thick felt markers.

In pairs, the group members lie down on a sheet of paper and their partner draws their outline onto the paper (not on their clothes!). They then swap roles and the other person has their outline drawn on a second sheet of paper. Then, each person paints in themselves into the outline. When finished, the self-portraits are Blu-tacked up round the room, and the group is invited to comment on their own drawings. Often the pictures offer insights into each individual's self-image, mood and attitude.

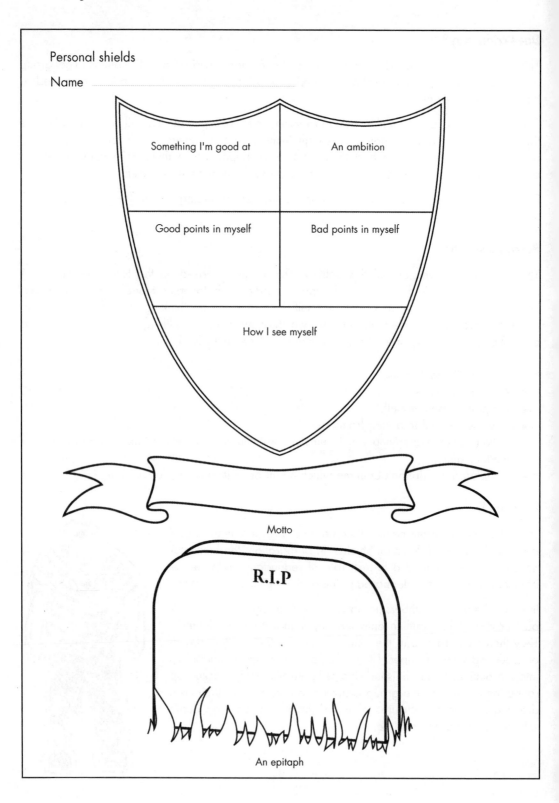

Personal shields

Name

Something I'm good at

An ambition

Good points in myself

Bad points in myself

How I see myself

Motto

R.I.P

An epitaph

Street orienteering

I first met up with this idea in the earlier version of Alan Smith's book, *Creative Outdoor Work with Young People* (1994). An outdoor activity which requires some preparation, it is best organised in pairs, and with older groups, and is obviously not suitable with any group you think might not come back!

My version has evolved a little differently than the other Alan's over the years. The aim is to get the group members used to working together co-operatively and to help them develop their personal observational and problem-solving skills. It is surprising how little many young people know about their own local patch.

In preparation, I photocopy a street map of the area I want to use, then 'white out' with Tippex or similar, some of the features and street names. Using this as a basis, I then walk around the area and devise a set of questions relating to specific points on the map. I number each question and put the number in a little circle on the map. The sort of questions I use are:

1. What is written over the doorway arch?
2. Who was born in this building?
3. Standing on this street corner, how many miles does it say that it is to Anytown on the signpost opposite?
4. What is on top of the church tower?
5. What colour is the animal in the pub sign?

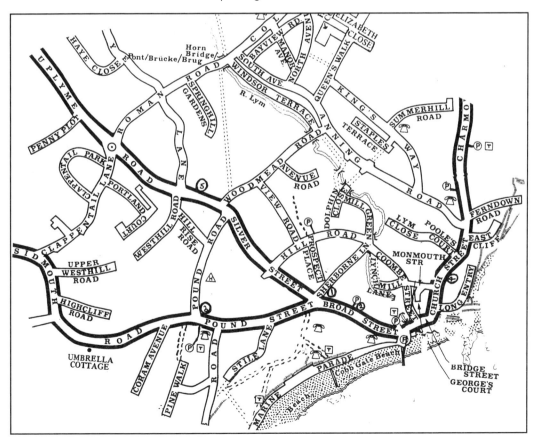

Obviously the organiser needs to provide an answer sheet for each pair, preferably on a clipboard, together with a copy of the map and a pen. It's also sensible to give a time for all of the pairs to return back to base.

These games and activities are only a 'taster' of the many that can be used effectively within a social groupwork programme with young people. It is well worth searching out some of these books, which can provide your work team with a more extensive 'toolkit' of resources.

References

Ball, K. et al. (1987) *Worth the risk?* SCF Hilltop, Yorkshire.

Ball, L. and Sowa, T. (1985) *Groupwork and I.T.* London Intermediate Treatment Association.

Booton, F. (1985) *Studies in Social Education 1860-1890.* Benfield Press.

Brandes, D. and Phillips, H. (1977) *Gamesters' Handbook.* Hutchinson.

Brandes, D. (1982) *Gamesters' 2.* Stanley Thorne.

Coles, B. et al. (1998) *Working with Young People on Estates.* Chartered Institute of Housing for oseph Rowntree Foundation.

Cooper, G. (1998) *Outdoors with Young People.* Russell House Publishing.

Cornell, J. B. (1987) *Listening to Nature.* Exley.

Dearling, A. and Armstrong, H. (1994) *New Youth Games Book.* Russell House Publishing.

Dearling, A. and Armstrong, H. (1995) *New Youth Arts and Craft Book.* Russell House Publishing.

Dearling, A. and Armstrong, H. (1996) *World Youth Games.* Russell House Publishing.

Dearling, A. with Armstrong, H. (1997) *Youth Action and the Environment.* Council for Environmental Education and Russell House Publishing.

Dynes, R. (1990) *Creative Games in Group Work.* Winslow Press.

Ekblom, P. (1998) *Community Safety and the Reduction and Prevention of Crime.* Home Office.

Institute of Social Inventions (1990) *Social Invention Workshops.* Institute of Social Inventions.

Jelfs, M. (1982) *The Manual for Action.* Action Resources Group.

Maclellan, G. (n.d.) *Talking to the Earth.* Capall Bann.

Paget, D. (1990) *The Art of Craft.* Cassell.

Platt, A. (1969) *The Child Savers: The Invention of Delinquency.* University of Chicago Press.

Priestley, P. and McGuire, J. (1983) *Learning to Help.* Tavistock.

Priestley, P. and McGuire, J. (1985) *Offending Behaviour.* Batsford.

Smith, A. (1994) *Creative Outdoor Work with Young People.* Russell House Publishing.

CHAPTER 6

Befriending

Alan Dearling

Introduction

Befriending is a common-sense idea that has been around a long time in community social work, and means rather different things in different places. Befriending is part of a continuum of models of one-to-one work with young people which can include peer tutoring, community social work, mentoring (see Chapter 12 on mentoring), and even tracking projects. One of the distinctions is that mentoring is usually more time-limited, involves joint work on action plans, and aims to achieve a measurable increase in knowledge, skills or improved behaviour on the part of the mentee. Befriending schemes tend to be longer term than mentoring interventions, and whilst mentors are expected to end their relationship with the mentee at the end of agreement, befriending is a more fluid, less formal arrangement that can often become the precursor to a natural, open-ended friendship. Both are aimed to offer support and encouragement for the young people involved. Befriending can also be a component part of a 'social action' approach to working with, and genuinely empowering, young people. There is no single definition for, or model of, befriending.

As well as being used in work with young people, the approach is now successfully used to support people with mental health problems, AIDS victims, carers, and older people who are socially isolated. One common aspect is that it typically involves members of the local community acting as 'volunteers', rather than on a paid basis, apart from expenses. Social work, as a relatively new profession, has often found this difficult to accommodate and it takes patience, commitment and more than a little 'bridge-building' on the part of befriending project staff and managers to build up the confidence of social services and other education and welfare agencies. Vic Blickem summed up the problems and the advantages very clearly in his foreword to *Developing an Alternative,* a report on the work of Cambridge Alternatives organisation. He headed the piece, *Professional Protectionism and Volunteers*:

> Volunteers were and continue to be crucial to the success of Cambridge Alternatives. It is they whom we primarily recruit and devote extensive training and support towards. They bring imagination, flexibility and talent to our range of work with young people . . . The disadvantage of this approach continues to be the attitude from some professionals that volunteers and IT workers are less professional than those workers with a Certificate of Qualification in Social Work . . . They who possess certain qualifications resist the non-professionals, because their recognition could be seen to cheapen the professional's credentials.
>
> (Blickem and Dearling, 1987)

What Cambridge Alternatives offered during the 1980s was a near-comprehensive range of community-based support services for young people in the Cambridge area. Befriending was one aspect of their service provision which also involved:

- Intermediate treatment groupwork as a direct alternative to residential or custodial care.
- Individual placement with Youthcare families and a range of other forms of supported accommodation.
- Counselling and advice services.
- Individually-tailored support programmes.
- Holiday and activity programmes.

In all it involved about 40 volunteers working with a group of full- and part-time paid staff.

One particular concern, which has become much more apparent in the move into the twenty-first century, is the need for police checks, and adequate support and training structures for recruiting, orienting and monitoring all volunteers, especially those involved in the relatively intense relationships which exist in befriending. Volunteers as a whole continue to be a valuable and beneficial resource, but with an increasing incidence of sexual and physical abuse scandals it would be foolhardy for youth work or social work agencies to recruit volunteer befrienders with a history of violence or abuse. However, it would be silly to throw this particular 'baby' out with the proverbial bath water. And that is especially true in 2001 and beyond, when befrienders are being increasingly used in work with older people, families, young people and people with a range of disabilities.

The recent Joseph Rowntree Foundation report, *Low Intensity Support: Preventing Dependency* (JRF, 1999) concludes that mobilising community involvement from volunteer befrienders and supporters is an ideal way in which to shift the focus from, 'crisis management' to 'crisis prevention'. Professional social workers will always have to grapple with issues such as 'objectivity', 'confidentiality' and 'detachment'. People in need of care and support, and that includes many young people, are looking for longer term friendship and commitment. Volunteer befrienders can often fill this gap. They also help people receiving the support to see it as a more natural form of help, relatively free from the stigmatisation and potential labelling inherent in receiving professional social work assistance. *A Friend Indeed* described the development of befriending for young carers, that is, young people who are still young, but help in the home as young carers. Their lives are 'often painful and distressing, made more so by neglect of family members, the local community and professionals who were paid to care' (Aldridge and Becker, 1994). Interestingly, the report clearly identified that the reality of 'growing up' for many young people actually involves their loss of childhood, and the imposition of significant adult responsibilities at a very young age. A young carer, Alison, from Nottingham summed up the need to have someone to talk to who would listen:

> It would be just like a best mate helping me wouldn't it? Once you'd got to know the person sort of thing: they'd know what you were on about and could be your friend for a long time.
>
> (Aldridge and Becker, 1994)

Here is one description of the befriending process:

> Befrienders are volunteers. Recent research suggests that people value the fact that others choose to spend time with them, rather than being under professional or family obligation to do so. Matching is the key to success. It is ideally based on shared interests, living near one another and similar personalities and ages. But selecting users can compound social exclusion if those thought 'difficult' are rejected.

Befriending relationships typically last over a year, which implies some success, and they are valued by those receiving the service. Volunteers also report benefits: improved job prospects, new leisure opportunities and wider social networks. A number of users would like to become volunteers in future. Befriending organisations encourage this to promote their inclusion in community life. (Dean and Goodlad, 1998)

Finding a successful model

The avoidance of stereotyping, paternalism and social work labelling are amongst the key ingredients in the most successful befriending schemes. Other aspects of befriending schemes which have been seen to work, include:

- *. . . meeting the needs of young people as adolescents rather than as delinquents.*
(Locke, 1983)
- *Volunteers have a particular imagination and creativity that's often lost in professional staff. They are generally more sympathetic and understanding of children's behaviour, with no set response and a great amount of flexibility.* (Blickem, in Blickem and Dearling, 1987)
- Work that can take place either in small groups or on a one-to-one basis, although some commentators like Ann Robinson have been more prescriptive about what it entails. She said:

For certain children, however, group work was not the answer . . . Thus, one-to-one schemes became one of the options available for children in trouble or at risk . . . befriending schemes are generally fairly informal (although, of course, well organised), usually activity based and aimed at enriching the child's social experience, but not specifically at 'reforming' delinquent children. (Robinson, 1986)

- It can provide a consistency of relationship for the young people involved, but if it goes wrong, it may become just another 'broken promise'.
- It can fill an emotional gap, and provide much needed attention and companionship.
- It may provide additional social and educational skill experiences.
- It can relieve the pressure on the parents and improve their relationship with their children, but care must be taken that the befriender does not become seen as a threat to the parents.
- *. . . provides disadvantaged, vulnerable children and young people with a supportive and challenging relationship with a caring adult.* (Rodger, 1994)
- It frequently complements other support and services which are provided by social services, youth and community services, education, health and housing departments.

Here is one example of befriending:

Neil's father died when he was 10 and during the last four years the boy has become increasingly inward-looking, solitary and often morose. Despite a caring mother, Neil's educational progress has become pitiful. In recent months he has committed a number of small offences and is now under supervision.

He has one interest: fishing. Until now he's gone fishing by himself, with makeshift equipment, but recently a keen angler, introduced by the social services department, has made friends with Neil, and suggested that two might fish together in waters set aside for the sport and where a licence is required.

Neil's mother has now bought the necessary licence, social services is meeting incidental expenses and the Intermediate Treatment Fund has provided funds for the a rod and other equipment: a classic example of befriending through the sharing of a mutual interest. Other befrienders in this locality have introduced youngsters in trouble to photography, natural history, cooking, upholstery, guitar playing and astronomy. (ITF, 1983)

What it is like to be befriended: Jimmy

This is an extract from *Fair Start: an observation of the Possilpark Befriending Project:*

> *Jimmy is 17. He's doing an HND course in computing at a city Further Education College. He did well at school: 4 Highers in English, Computing, Physics and Chemistry and 7 Standard Grades. 'Not good enough to get intae university, but . . .'*

> *He tells me he's been on Social Work supervision for the last 7 years. He doesn't know his dad – wouldn't recognise him on the street – and has lived with his aunt, separate from his mum and 4 brothers since he was 10. 'My aunt told me my mum wanted me to stay with her so I could get out of the children's home'.*

> *Why had he been taken into care? Jimmy describes himself as having been 'a bit of a tearaway'. He had 'behavioural difficulties' at primary school. He had trouble at home but he can't remember what that was. His social worker put him forward for befriending.*

> *His befriender is Rhona. He's been seeing her for a few months. She's a student at the university. He thinks she's in her twenties. They go to the cinema. 'I'm meeting a lot of different people through Rhona. Like students, people from different parts of the world, people with different attitudes. I treat Rhona more as a friend than a social worker'. Jimmy has recently moved out of his aunt's and is now staying in digs with a landlady organised by social work.*

> *'I don't make friends easily. Normally I stay in at weekends. I don't go to clubs or anything: I can't dance . . . I know I can be quite annoying . . . the way I'm going just now, I'll die a lonely old man' . . .*

> *One of the major problems seems to be that if it weren't for Rhona, he would have only acquaintances, not friends at college, and his lonely room and (computer) at nights.*
> (Rodger, 1994)

Group befriending in Stockton

What follows is a description of one of the youth befriending groups run by the Eastern Ravens Trust, a project in Stockton on Tees, Cleveland, which developed an extensive programme based on the use of 'group befriending'. It is by no means the only model, but the enthusiasm and commitment shown by the staff and volunteers are clearly evident and may provide ideas for future 'preventive' provision in the youth justice system.

This has been edited from a special report that Alan Dearling put together for *IT News* in 1984. At the time, the Trust had been in operation for over 20 years and pioneered the use of volunteers in offering long-term group befriending to nearly a hundred young people a year who lived in poor social housing stock. In an average year, about a dozen groups were run, involving over thirty volunteers providing weekly activity and discussion 'clubs' for youngsters aged between eight and eighteen. Most of these groups were viewed as long term. They were never established on the basis of social work referrals, nor were they youth justice groups. Instead they were operated on an ethos developed by Eastern Ravens over the years, of providing a bit of extra support, care, love, experience and opportunity in the lives of the local young people.

Their model for working

Their befriending work always operated through groups, which normally included between five and nine young people in them. They ran as an informal, but regular meeting for most of the youngsters' school lives. The girls' group described here existed for seven years. Alongside this long term provision, the Trust operated summer holiday groups, which accepted youngsters thought to have special needs and referred by the County Psychological Service. The aim of these summer holiday groups was similar in many respects. Marion Stockton, one of the co-ordinators, reported the view of one psychologist:

> . . . in some cases Eastern Ravens became a lifeline for families, where six weeks of unrelieved tension would probably have led to failure to function and perhaps reception into care.

To set the context for the work, and as an indication of how the Trust viewed its own philosophy of operations, a portion of the Director, Keith Lindsey's comments are reprinted first:

> Eastern Ravens fills a vital gap in the overall provision for young people. The statutory youth service and traditional voluntary organisations increasingly (though by no means exclusively) serve the needs of many well-adjusted young people. This is an invaluable though limited role. The social services department primarily responds to those youngsters who are already in trouble. The 1982 Criminal Justice Act seems to be designed to make the disposal of the young offender more punitive and is therefore likely to concentrate the focus of attention of social services and probation upon those young people who are already offending. There is therefore a vacuum because there is a lack of resources made available for work with those youngsters who find themselves without any real sense of purpose and who with a little bit of help could be diverted away from trouble and enabled to make more sense of life. The scope for such work is very great and pockets of increased determination particularly at practitioner level to respond to those who make their needs conspicuous, for example, through becoming glue sniffers, are encouraging. (Dearling, 1984)

If this sounds at all familiar, it should be, since restorative justice is based on the need for a range of interventions, including the need to decrease the amount of 'labelled' social work taking place. The style of work organised by Eastern Ravens' Trust was particularly interesting, in that it offered alternatives to the more typical models of both groupwork and individual befriending projects, which are more familiar across the UK.

Swainby Road girls' group

Background

At the heart of this group was one woman's concern for one girl. Linda McGarvey lived in Swainby Road and was worried about one girl, Julie, who lived nearby. Julie had experienced problems with friends making fun of her and was attending an ESN school. Linda had found that two other girls who lived close by were the only ones who did not mock Julie. Consequently, with encouragement from Eastern Ravens, Linda invited the three girls to become a group – a sort of private youth club, calling round to Linda's house on a regular night each week. The girls, together with Linda, played games together and did some baking. It was all very low-key, but it offered new experiences when they all went out together for activities like skating, and a chance to meet a different adult. Two years on, the group was increased in number to five and Dave helped Linda as a second leader and was then joined by Terri. Later that same year a major staff change occurred when Linda, Dave and Terri handed over adult leadership of the group to Elizabeth and Fiona. These ladies continued with the group for a further four years, when the group took the decision to disband. The leadership change had coincided with an increase in the size of the group to seven, and all the girls stayed with the leaders until the final party which effectively marked the end of virtually an era in their shared lives. When the group broke up, the girls' ages ranged from fifteen and a half up to nineteen.

What the group did

Unlike structured social work groups, the meetings were not regularly recorded or monitored throughout the life of the group. Nor were there strict grounds for referral. The girls were mostly somewhat shy and rather introvert. They didn't have much chance of getting out of their homes, with no youth club locally, and in general they were not a 'problem' group. Dave and a student originally visited the schools attended by the girls and noted that the girls were 'scarcely known by anyone.' It was this sense of isolation, and, the girls' boredom and lack of stimulation that the adult leaders sought to overcome. Elizabeth told me:

> The girls seemed to have no outlook on life and their lives seemed almost pre-determined, leading inevitably to marriage and children.

She went on to say that:

> . . . the discussions and activities undertaken by the group were designed to add a bit of variety to their lives, and to show the girls that there was more to life.

The activities themselves were often exactly the same as are offered in the programmes of many youth clubs and intermediate treatment groups. Snooker, pool, table tennis, football, jewellery-making, discussions, trips out to the swimming pool, skating and summer holidays were all part of the programme. Very little money was supplied by Eastern Ravens Trust to their groups. In the mid 1980s it was only £18 per month, and the groups were expected to pay 20 pence per mile back to the organisation for the use of transport: a fact resented by many of the adult staff. The groups themselves raised all other funding for activities and holidays. The girls group each paid a weekly 'sub' for attending the group's club nights, as they called them, and raised money by organising jumble sales, raffles etc. These ventures were seen as group activities, and useful exercises designed to give confidence to the girls. The staff all commented to me that the groups needed a bit more money from somewhere to improve the range of experiences, though not 'too generous' but should 'allow groups to try activities they might not be able to experience.' For example, the girls had at one time planned to go horse-riding, but were unable to afford the cost.

However, over the seven years, especially through the group holidays, they were able to visit places, they had never even heard of, let alone visited before. The group seem to have enjoyed all their holidays, but particular mention was made of visits to the Scottish Borders.

How successful was the group?

Three of the girls told me that the group had helped them 'come out of themselves'. Certainly the three girls I met, all spoke clearly on why the group had been important in their lives. They said that it had kept them 'off the street' and 'out of mischief'. They also spoke of looking forward to seeing their friends each week and learning to succeed at activities like skating. The fourth and original member of the group, Julie, seemed to have gained most, through being made to feel wanted by the other girls and becoming more confident.

The fact that it was a 'girls' group' was important to the girls. Tracey and Dawn told me that they were able to talk about different things, and enjoy lots of activities without having to take second place because boys were present. This caused, to some extent, a difficult period in the life of the group, when they collectively decided not to allow a male helper to join them. The girls told me that it was their wish at that time to only have female staff with them. One of the mothers, said that she thought it would have been a bit peculiar to have a man working with the group and this may have influenced the girls when this decision was made. Dave had been a leader with the group, but he said he thought he would have found it increasingly difficult as the girls grew older.

Staff and premises

None of the adults involved with the Swainby girls' group were professional youth or social workers. Eastern Ravens was used by a lot of adults to gain experience in doing youth and community work, and Elizabeth said that working with the group gave her the impetus to apply for a full-time social work course. All the staff said that they benefited from the group as well as it giving opportunities to the girls. Because the group lasted for seven years, there might have been a worry that the girls would become dependent on the group. This was, according to Elizabeth, true, although she described it as an interdependence, with the women and girls needing one another. Dave expressed it differently, saying that the girls were dependent on the activities, but not the staff.

Different adults saw themselves, and were seen by the girls in different roles. One girl said, perceptively, that Elizabeth was 'leader' and that Fiona was one of her 'helpers'. This mixing of styles amongst staff is quite common in Eastern Ravens, and Fiona occupied more of a 'big sister' position in the group, while Elizabeth acted as a leader and perhaps a 'mum'. Linda, on the other hand, had become involved partly because the girls were her neighbours, unlike Elizabeth who lived five miles away. Linda's husband Kenny had already been a leader for another Eastern Ravens' group and was himself a member of the first group from twenty years before. The backgrounds of the staff involved in the group varied from accountant, betting shop worker, through secretary to trainee social worker, and this was indicative of the broad range of Eastern Ravens Trust volunteers. The fact that staff changed, but the group stayed together is also unusual in groupwork. The girls said that they had liked and got on with all the staff. Linda and Dave said the change of staffing '. . . was good: it brought new ideas into the group'.

The premises used by the group were varied. Linda had used her own front room, as did Elizabeth later in the life of the group. The girls also met at the Eastern Ravens' Club Hut, the IT centre and the social work community house before it was demolished. This was in addition to trips out, which were increasingly planned by the whole group for the week ahead. This variety of settings for the meetings probably reinforced the view of the girls that it was 'our night' and 'our private youth club'. Eastern Ravens as an organisation, played little part in these weekly meetings and outings to such diverse venues as a Shakin' Steven's concert or an Old People's Home. Though in the background, Eastern Ravens Trust Director Keith, was perceived by the girls as, '. . . he makes all the big decisions on who does what'. A quiet role in fact, but, like the girls' group and others run in Stockton an important part of many youngsters' lives.

Some end notes

The examples in this section show some of the diversity of what 'befriending' can offer. It doesn't easily fit into a professionalised model of social work, or anti-crime intervention. Rather it seems to work most successfully when it is based on a natural, community-based form of self-help and voluntary caring. To quote from the JRF (1999) report:

> *The fundamental lesson for policy-makers, at a national or local level, is a common sense one. Prevention is better than cure. It is cheaper and more effective to provide low intensity support services* (such as befriending) *than to allow situations to deteriorate until people need high intensity/residential care. If they follow agendas that people set for themselves, low intensity support services improve the quality of people's lives; increase the degree of their social inclusion; and promote choice and control over how their needs are defined and met.*
>
> (JRF, 1999)

On its own, befriending is not an answer to youth offending. However, it is a complementary means of providing additional resources and support for young people, using adult members of the community in a non-stigmatising role. Befrienders can even help to free up resources from YOTs and the like, and provide a little helpful support and empathy, where and when it is needed. As Derek Rodger wryly comments at the end of the *Fair Start* report on the Possilpark scheme:

> *Unlike most of the health, care and education jobs in the country where people have responsibility for children, these* (selection and training processes) *include police checks. 'In six years', said Brian Wright holding the table, 'we've had no disasters.' As my gaze looks over his shoulder, out the window and over the rooftops of this stricken urban landscape towards the Campsie hills to the north of the city, the real disaster is in front of our eyes.*
>
> (Rodger, 1994)

References

Aldridge, J. and Becker, S. (1994) *A Friend Indeed: The Case for Befriending Young Carers.* Young Carers Research Group, Loughborough University.

Blickem, V. and Dearling, A. (1987) *Developing an Alternative: Community Help for Young People.* Cambridge Alternatives.

Dean, J. and Goodlad, R. (1998) *Supporting Community Participation? The Role and Impact of Befriending.* Pavilion Publishing with Joseph Rowntree Foundation.

Dearling, A. (1984) Group Befriending in Stockton. *IT News*. April.

Intermediate Treatment Fund (1983) *Youngsters in Trouble: The Way Ahead*. Vision Associates.

Joseph Rowntree Foundation (1999) *Low Intensity Support: Preventing Dependency*. Joseph Rowntree Foundation.

Locke, T. (1983) *Cambridge: The Community-Rooting of Intermediate Treatment*. National Youth Bureau.

Robinson, A. (1986) *Befriending and Tracking Schemes*. National Children's Bureau.

Rodger, D. (1994) *Fair Start: An Observation of the Possilpark Befriending Project*. Argyll Publishing/Save the Children.

Stockton, M. (1984) A Shared Commitment in Response to a Need. *IT News*. April.

CHAPTER 7

Working away from base

Alan Dearling

This chapter is largely based on material I produced while working as Training Officer for the Scottish Intermediate Treatment Resource Centre, though up-dated and amended with reference to a range of more recent publications. It is intended as a brief introduction to some of the guidelines and aspects of programme planning which are useful points of reference for anyone organising trips, courses and residential periods for young people. Your own local authority or organisation will probably have its own practice guidelines, which you should make sure you are familiar with and adhere to.

Why go away from base?

The answer is very simple. The process of planning a trip away, travelling to a venue, sharing in everything from cooking to activities like walking, canoeing, horse-riding and orienteering is full of potential for:

- building relationships between adults and group members
- opportunities for developing confidence, self-awareness, leadership and self-reliance
- learning new skills and experiencing new activities
- empowerment
- developing awareness of, and respect for, the environment
- developing group cohesion yet at the same time allowing individuals to learn about themselves

In youth justice work, the opportunity to go away together with a group of young people can offer both adults and young people the chance to temporarily forget their everyday roles and lives, and allow for the development of a more positive lifestyle. However, there is a large **but** hovering on the horizon of this particular type of venture. Because of a number of high profile disasters that have struck outdoor pursuits type youth groups, there is ever increasing resistance on the part of some organisations to 'take a risk' and engage in potentially hazardous activities and experiences.

A second worry that frightens off some youth justice organisations from involvement in activities and trips, is the fear of arousing controversy and criticism for giving 'treats' to offenders. There's no easy answer. If you look at the following excerpts from my own diaries of trips away from base with West Coast Adventure, you can perhaps begin to perceive the potential benefits for young people, their families and the communities they normally live in. But, if you're organising a programme of external activities, don't expect it to be easy, or, to put it in different words, Hamish Murphy, from Wester Hailes Youth Programme in Edinburgh, suggests:

Wester Hailes is an adventurous place. The local residents want to come to terms with troubled and troublesome young people. Young people themselves want adventurous activities. Local agencies want to involve local residents and young people in positive activities. The recipe is a troubled sea. Waves of professional jargon, whirlpools of labelling, eddies of unmet needs.

A different kind of outdoor adventure course

Richard and Chuck run about a dozen adventure courses per year at West Coast Adventure. Sometimes both of them are involved, on other occasions they work independently, Richard Shuff using the uninhabited island of Scarba as a base for one week and longer courses, and Chuck Whitehead commencing his 'adventures' from Lismore. Highland Region staff and the Kinmylies Children's Centre in Inverness have been using the West Coast Adventure organisation for a number of years. The mere mention of outdoor pursuits conjures up images of hearty adults with red flushed cheeks cajoling recalcitrant youngsters up mountains. The West Coast Adventure organisation offers something rather different and certainly of more use to youth justice type projects. Chuck told me: 'We're not just hanging people over an abseil; we're interested in people'.

Survival for real

Their programme of activities evolved over ten years of experience of outdoor activities work with young people. Chuck had previously worked as senior course director at Brathay Hall in Cumbria, where many of the early youth justice groups run by David Thorpe and David Smith from Lancaster University were brought for residential periods. Richard's background includes using 'survival skills for real' in the SAS and training as a PE teacher. He also worked with John Ridgway for a number of years planning and running survival-type courses and expeditions.

What constitutes an adventure?

The aims of their particular adventure course coincide with two key 'group work' aims of all youth justice work. They are:
1. To give individuals varied opportunities for success and achievement.
2. To give the whole group an exciting and new experience together.

How this is achieved depends to a great extent on the way in which staff make each Adventure course flexible and responsive to the needs of particular individuals and groups. Before groups come to a course either Chuck or Richard visits the organisation sponsoring the course. Plans are made concerning possible activities, food, types of accommodation and how the youngsters can be fully involved in the course decision-making. This is essential in the way the courses are structured and it was obvious during my own stay on Lismore that West Coast Adventurers practise what they preach: which, unfortunately, is not always the case in youth work!

The length of the courses varies from four days upwards with one youngster recently spending 20 days on Scarba taking part in three successive courses. The course I visited comprised four boys from a group based in Invergordon. For reasons of confidentiality their names are altered in my account of the group's activities. In talking to me they chose their own pseudonyms: Fergus, Byrtle, Henry and Ronnie (chosen because of Ronnie Biggs, would you believe!). Ronnie had already survived a trip to Scarba, so as an 'old hand' was experienced in a number of the survival tactics and activities. The Invergordon course was only a short four day affair, so a structure was devised to enable all the participants to try as much as possible. Usually Highland Region groups would send two staff with their groups as a minimum, but on this occasion only one worker, John, was able to be with the group. The involvement of adults from the home communities is seen as an integral part of each course since it allows relationships to be built or strengthened and for trust to develop. Assessments are made of young people attending these courses and according to all the social workers I have talked to, the positive gains are enormous. Workers have seen young people in a range of situations, under stress and in positions of responsibility; these experiences allow for more accurate insights, and better assessments and recommendations.

The course I was visiting gave the participants the opportunity to experience:

- sailing in a 32ft. yacht
- abseiling
- swimming
- fishing
- hill-walking
- rough camping including in a cave
- canoeing
- camp cooking

Chuck told me how he tried to find places to visit and stay in that 'don't feel used'. The remoteness, the absence of shops and amenities and the reliance for support and friendship on other members of the group are part of the groupwork process that is quickly developed under Chuck's supportive guidance. I found that the gentle support which Chuck gave to us all as individuals whether it was while we were canoeing or cooking made it easy for other barriers to be dropped. Certainly, all the adults running youth justice-type groups who have used the Adventure courses seem to be universally impressed with the consistent adult support offered by the West Coast Adventure team.

I had also encountered this when Hilary and Margaret had introduced themselves to the boys on board their boat *Tamara*. They said:

We don't want to know what you've done back home. We want to give you new experiences and if you treat us well we will do the same. If you give us a hard time, we can make your time hard as well.

Hilary and Margaret have sailed this boat all over the world and being retired and from very different backgrounds than the boys, it was fascinating to see them getting to know each other. Byrtle and Henry were in the first sailors' expedition along with John, one of their group workers. They learned how to steer the boat, something about setting sails, rowing the rubber dinghy and fishing. When we all met up on the Saturday afternoon Henry and Byrtle were full of enthusiasm, telling me about their exploits, successes and how they had got up at six am for a long hike and a swim prior to a morning's sailing.

Fergus, Ronnie, Chuck and myself had the shared experience of tinned haggis cooked on meths burners, and some interesting conversations about Invergordon, the islands, alcohol, drugs and being in an I.T. group. This was followed by a few creepy tales in the darkness of a very damp, dark, hard cave. Not the most pleasant night's sleep for any of us, punctuated by bats, large drips of water falling onto our muddy sleeping bags and Fergus yelling out, 'This place is the pits!' a bit too loudly. Breakfast and a surprisingly sunny start soon repaired any after-cave-sleeping blues and a co-operative meal was followed by more canoeing and hiking back to Port na Moralachd. Swimming was ruled out by the presence of multitudes of nasty looking jellyfish, but the company for a short while of five dolphins close into shore made everyone smile.

Why do it?

This sort of adventure course is rather unique because of the people co-ordinating it. They have all the necessary practical skills in outdoor pursuits, and well maintained equipment,

but, more importantly, they have a natural empathy with the young people, and a solid understanding of groupwork practice. They work closely with the referring agency staff and are very flexible. With staff from Kinmylies they work out assessment reports on the young people, and adult staff, and these are used to allow the group members to be involved in the most appropriate future schemes. The relationships built up on the adventure courses are of paramount importance back in the communities from where the youngsters come. Both Henry and Byrtle told me they hoped to continue some of the activities on their own back in their home area. All four boys were very proud of what they had managed to achieve for themselves and of how they had overcome many personal fears. I was conscious of this especially when Byrtle said to me, 'During the number of years I've been in trouble I've learned never to trust anyone, however many years of experience they have. I'm pertified of abseiling, but I still want to try it here'. Ronnie talked to me a lot about the dreadful weather when he had done his '20 days' and made nettle soup, slept in three caves and battled off Scarba's entire adder population single-handed. Well, something like that, anyway!

The West Coast Adventure team are very keen that they do not become building-based in their approach. In most of their courses, members of the group may never go inside a building. They also do not own tents, which is a conscious decision to place emphasis on survival techniques, and individual and group resourcefulness. The only possible problem with this approach is in making the adventures too tough and too demanding for adult staff from the sponsoring agency. The unaggressive style used by the West Coast Adventure team, 'taking folk as they come', works with most young people from youth justice groups. Tom Sloan from Grampian Social Work department told me that for his group, the adventure course had been 'the high point of the summer holidays'. Highland Region staff agreed and were firmly committed to building the courses into their groupwork programmes whenever it is appropriate. The benefits seem to be significantly greater than those gained through self-organised outdoor pursuits programmes.

Planning

Proper care and concern about safety is vital, but there are many other aspects of planning to consider as well. If a weekend, week, or even longer away is being considered, you will need to book up well in advance, since many centres, camps and outdoor facilities are used all the year round, or, are only open for limited periods of the year. Before confirming actual bookings there are a few things to bear in mind:

- The most important issue is how, and to what extent, the young people will be involved in planning for the residential experience. Ideally, the group should be involved in all relevant aspects of planning and preparation. This could include choice of venue, type of accommodation (centre, tents, caravan, hostel, etc.), mode of transport, activity planning, catering arrangements etc. There will, however, be times when the total involvement of the young people in all aspects of planning will be neither relevant nor practical. For example, residential accommodation may have to be booked before the group is formed, in which case it is usual to explain to the group the reason why they have not been consulted about this particular aspect of decision making. Generally though, the involvement of young people in group decision making of this nature is a useful element in groupwork and personal social educations.

- Are the premises suitable for the particular group? For example, can the centre cope with:
  - a mixed group
  - adolescents
  - people from a variety of ethnic backgrounds etc.?
- What equipment, such as bedding, kitchen utensils, crockery are provided? What else is needed?
- What facilities are there indoors if the weather fails?
- What programme possibilities for activities exist in the area around the centre?
- Are there any rules, regulations or expectations which may affect your choice?

It is advisable to check on these things with the warden or the organisation who manages the centre before making a definite commitment.

Staffing considerations

Not all staff who work successfully with young people in day-to-day meetings in youth justice work will be able to adapt to working away from base. This can be for a variety of reasons. It may be age, adaptability, lack of skills in an outdoor setting, or just their preference *not* to do this type of work. In terms of selecting the balance of staff to go with a particular group of young people, it is important to consider:

- Their experience and qualifications in the activities likely to be undertaken (and where applicable, how these complement those held by any staff at the centres to be used.
- Their levels of fitness.
- The need for a balance by gender and experience.
- Their knowledge of first aid and safety and emergency procedures.

To prepare staff, some training may be required, including familiarisation with the Department for Education's *Safety Guidelines for Outdoor Education*, and to help protect the environment, *The Country Code*.

Guidelines for youth group residential periods

Occasional problems will always arise when running residential groups, but some can be avoided by using common sense plus adhering to the guidelines given below.

Examples of problems that can occur during trips away, include incidents involving damage to property, theft, and group members getting lost. These guidelines are intended as a basis from which, if an incident does occur during a residential period, management and workers will have mutual confidence in dealing with the repercussions of the incident. In youth justice work, groups will probably include a number of disturbed children who have difficulties with authority and needs for 'acting-out'. It must be realised therefore, that despite impeccable professional actions by workers, occasional incidents will occur on group trips away from base.

Returning to a thorny issue: risk-taking is an integral part of the groupwork process. The added risks involved in anything from abseiling to white water rafting are only another aspect of the risk-taking which is a part of every youth justice/youth worker's function. The management of these trips and residentials must reflect this fact. Workers should therefore be aware of the potential for problems, confrontation and even violence, and should maintain their normal professional practice for working with vulnerable and possibly disruptive young people, for example:

- attempting to defuse aggression
- avoidance of damage to other people or property
- awareness of the group's and individuals' whereabouts and actions as far as reasonably possible etc.

Certain activities require young people to operate in teams, pairs or on their own, and constant 24 hours a day supervision by adults will not be feasible or desirable. The group and individuals will also need time away from the adults as a normal human requirement. This is all part of the development of trust and responsibility that group work with young people is about. To achieve this, the group must be allowed to discuss and experience these concepts, in accordance with the workers' professional judgement. Furthermore, painful experience has shown that where a group feels that it is constantly being 'policed', incidents and damage can be guaranteed.

Accountability and safety

The usual system of working with youth justice groups, and similar, is for the staff team to accept joint responsibility for the work done with the group. Since one of the principal aims is often to develop the group's attitudes to authority and responsibility, this model is seen as the most appropriate in leading the group towards more mature ways of dealing with authority.

Therefore, before undertaking a residential period, the staff team should be absolutely clear as to whether joint accountability is the accepted model or whether a recognised individual is 'in charge' for the trip away. In both cases, the member of staff should be named on the parental consent forms, though only in the first case have they a line of communication with management on issues of accountability.

Sadly, accidents can happen. In the area where I am based, what became known as the 'Lyme Bay canoe tragedy' occurred when a series of poor decisions were made by the staff of an outdoor residential centre. Professional staffing depends on minimising risks through adopting appropriate codes of conduct relating to the types of activity being undertaken. For instance, a scuba diving qualification is not necessary for taking a group to the seaside, but having someone with a life-saving qualification might be deemed appropriate.

Before the residential period

1. Workers should obtain the necessary consent forms from parents or guardians allowing the child to participate in both the residential period and in any potentially dangerous activities that might be undertaken. Forms should also indicate any special medical requirements.
2. For ease and continuity of communication, the same worker should sign any written applications (e.g. holiday application forms, booking forms, letters of information etc.) and should liaise with the outdoor centre, other facilities likely to be used, the caretaker, etc. The decision on who undertakes this should be done with reference to the paragraph accountability' above.

3. The 'nature' of the group, that is whether it is a youth justice group, or whatever, should be clearly described in any verbal discussion or written application to book an outdoor centre, camp site or residential facility.
4. Workers should ascertain the location of the nearest doctor and hospital to the centre. An adequate first aid kit should be taken by the workers on the trip.
5. The workers should, if possible, visit the centre and area under consideration, before the trip, to acquaint themselves with the layout, resources, staff and suitability. It should be noted that a very plush centre may inhibit some groups, and that a dilapidated one may encourage minor acts of vandalism on the grounds that 'one more bit is not going to make much difference'.
6. Equipment such as tents, canoes and sports equipment should be checked for safety.
7. Workers should discuss with the group before the period, any rules which the centre, the workers, or the group wish observed.

On arrival
1. Workers should undertake a complete inspection of the interior and immediate exterior of the accommodation, noting any damage. This should preferably be done with the warden or caretaker.
2. Any rules, limitations and obligations should be clarified with the warden and explained at the soonest opportunity to the group, if it is not already aware of them.
3. Free access to fire escapes should be ensured.
4. Workers should maintain a written daily record of the group's activities and any problems which occur, indicating the time, people involved and circumstances of any incidents.

On departure
1. Workers must again undertake a complete inspection of the interior and immediate exterior, noting any damage. This should preferably be done with the warden or caretaker.
2. Workers should attempt to leave the centre in the condition in which it was found (or better).

Afterwards
1. It is important to hold at least one debriefing session after a trip away. This can deal both with any problems and with any potential for future trips and activities.
2. Individuals should be provided with opportunities to build upon their experiences.

Boundary management and programme planning

To maximise the usefulness of youth residential experiences in groupwork practice it is useful (if not essential) to spend time before the residential trip in defining the boundaries relating to standards of group decision making, behaviour, and participation in activities and life tasks. All are equally important. It is crucial that all group members (both adults and young people) have a shared awareness of group boundaries and established norms before embarking on what can be an intense and demanding group experience. Work on boundary management issues must take into account the accommodation and environment within which the group will be living, e.g. tents, caravan, residential centre, urban or country location etc.

Adequate preparation of the group can forestall major problems arising over relatively minor issues, e.g. one staff member allowing young people to smoke in the centre and another member of staff objecting on principle to this position.

It is useful to have at least some of your programme worked out before your departure, always taking the weather and safety into consideration. This may entail pre-booking activities or equipment: you cannot depend on going pony trekking, for example, when you arrive, and you may not be the only people who want to do it on a particular Saturday afternoon. If you know that there is a swimming pool, riding stables, park, funfair, ice rink, cinema, boating pond or whatever, then you can involve the group in programme planning beforehand and be sure of what you can and cannot do when you're there.

It is also helpful if before you go you are aware of the opening times of, for example, cinema, swimming pool, ice rink – remember also that some of these facilities might be seasonal only. A few minutes on the telephone to the centre and the local Tourist Information Centre, or local council offices, can save a great deal of heartache later on. Take the natural environment into consideration when thinking of programming. Proximity to hills, the sea, forest parks, historical sites, resorts, can all provide suitable material for your itinerary. If you know of any other groups who have used a particular centre, have a chat with them; they might be able to help you a lot.

Before you go make sure you have thought of everything; it's too late when you get there.

Have you:

- Confirmed your booking and paid any necessary deposit?
- Booked your transport, making sure it's big enough, is roadworthy, insured, taxed, MOTed and checked on any regulations regarding drivers, insurance etc?
- Arranged for equipment: sleeping bags and inners, crockery, cutlery, cooking utensils, suitable outdoor clothing for the activities planned, activity equipment, first aid kit, small games for indoors?
- Worked out a draft programme and pre-booked facilities or activities where necessary?
- Bought enough food and worked out a balanced menu and meals plan? Checked with the group concerning any special diets?
- Obtained parental consents and filled in any necessary forms to conform to organisational procedures where applicable?
- Ascertained that adequate insurance cover has been provided?
- Allowed enough money for petrol and any activities planned? Always have a contingency fund if possible.
- Prepared the group by informing them of any special clothing, etc., they will need? Drawn up an equipment list with the youth group? Include radio, musical instruments, arts and crafts and sports equipment etc. on such a list.
- Confirmed that all the staff are available for the camp?
- Ascertained any medical history that may require one of your group to have special medications on hand? It helps if you know where the nearest doctor to the centre can be found.
- Liaised with any staff (or caretaker or manager) at the residential centre about rules, so that these can be discussed by staff and young people prior to the trip?

If you have done all of these things and made suitable sacrifices to the gods in respect of the weather, you should be able to spend the trip away participating fully with your group and not running about in circles avoiding disasters. Going away with groups should be good fun, stimulating and memorable: if that is what you plan for, that's probably what you'll get. Positive social education includes enjoying yourselves!

Licensing

Since October 1997, under the Activity Centres (Young Persons' Safety) Act 1995, providers of many adventure activities have to undergo inspection of their safety management systems. The scheme does not apply to schools and colleges working with their own pupils; voluntary youth groups or activities where the young people are accompanied by their own parents or guardians. Most climbing, watersports, trekking and caving activities run for commercial gain fall into the remit of the scheme. The Adventure Activities Licensing Authority is based at 17 Lambourne Crescent, Llanishen, Cardiff CF14 5GF.

Further reading

I'd strongly recommend the following books to anyone aiming to develop their knowledge of working away from base with young people. They offer much more detailed information on environmental education, planning and sustainability, resource information, as well as many activities which have proven to be successful with a variety of youth groups and ages.

References

Cooper, G. (1998) *Outdoors with Young People.* Russell House Publishing.

Nicholls, D. (1995) *Employment Practice and Policies in Youth and Community Work.* Russell House Publishing.

Smith, A. (1994) *Creative Outdoor Work with Young People.* Russell House Publishing.

Information on the Licensing scheme is contained in: *Guidance to the Licensing Authority on the Adventure Activities Licensing Regulations 1996.* Health and Safety Executive Books.

See also:
DfEE *Safety Guidelines for Outdoor Education.* DfEE.
The Country Code. HMSO.

CHAPTER 8

Volunteers

Alan Dearling

Introduction

The concept of volunteering has a long and disparate past in the whole range of 'people services'. Since the services provided for, and with, young people discussed in this compendium have evolved principally from youth work, social work, probation and education, it seems reasonable to offer some illustrations of how these services have at times struggled with the use of volunteers, and part-time staff generally, and often greatly benefited from their involvement. Historically, a secondary, but equally important aspect of voluntary engagement in the development of services has involved the establishment of 'voluntary agencies', at local and national level, as opposed to individual volunteers working in projects. Voluntary agencies have often produced some of the most innovative examples of what used to be known as intermediate treatment (IT) and youth social work, but have also fuelled the debate about 'whose responsibility' crime prevention and youth delinquency work is. One example of such criticism was aired in the 1991 Barnardo's report, *Just Deserts or Just Growing up?* where the authors reported that:

> In Liverpool, the quality of service which Barnardo's could finance, at a time when local authority cutbacks and major local controversies and difficulties, was contrasted with what was certainly perceived as less well-resourced local authority provision . . . the fear was that voluntary sector involvement had led to inequities in service provision across the city.

By the 1990s an increasing amount of the work in community based services with young offenders had become 'contracted out', being financed by a range of government and even European funds, but managed by national and local voluntary agencies such as Save the Children Fund, Barnardo's, INCLUDE, the Prince's Trust, NCH-Action for Children, Cities in Schools, NACRO and many others.

The question of **who** should be encouraged to work with young people in settings such as youth clubs, youth justice schemes or groupwork programmes of various kinds is seen as problematic. The considerations which frequently come into play (and you may wish to modify these as a checklist for your work) include:

- How do you recruit volunteers?
- What is the age of the person?
- Have they ever been in trouble or involved in crime?
- What experience do they have of working with young people?
- What skills can they bring to a scheme?
- Do they have any accredited qualifications?
- Are they willing to undertake formal training?

- Will they be able to fit in with the existing team?
- What relationships do they have with the young people involved?
- Are they 'local' to the community?

And, more generally:
- Should they be paid for their work or be fully 'voluntary' in their involvement?
- How does use of volunteers impact on the running of a 'professional' service?
- In what ways does the use of volunteers help to empower young people?
- How can volunteers be involved in the management and running of work with young people?
- How can issues relating to sexism and racism be best tackled?
- In what ways can community involvement in community safety schemes with young people occur?

The debates surrounding volunteers and volunteering are by no means new, for instance, the notion of young people being a threat to their elders through involvement in managing projects. In 1863, Arthur Sweatman reported that one of the members at the monthly tea meeting of the London Working Men's Clubs:

> . . . urged the great importance of not allowing any member under twenty five to be on the committee; otherwise, as was the case at one time in the Club he belonged to, the youths might get completely the upper hand and do great mischief.   (reprinted in Booton, 1985)

As new professions such as social work develop they are inevitably going to question the involvement in this workplace, of people who are less formally qualified. This has created a number of conflicts and contradictions in the development of community based initiatives in the broad arena of crime prevention. Comparatively, the myriad range of organisations involved in providing youth and community services has most often stressed the positive advantages of involving volunteers in work with young people. In 1984, the National Youth Bureau published the report, *Starting from Strengths*. It was a review of the training needs of part-time youth and community workers. It strikes us that the issues that report raised are still central today. It contended that training for part-time and volunteer staff only becomes positive when:

- *It leads to an increase in their confidence and self-esteem and provides them with the opportunity to prove their own worth and skills to themselves.*
- *Participants' experience and strengths are 'recruited' by the trainer so as to build up a feeling that each has something to contribute.*
- *It is consistently related to the day-to-day practice of those involved and takes into account the difficulties and problems they face.*   (Butters, 1984)

As you can see from the above, the report was couched in somewhat inaccessible language, but had a significant effect on how volunteers were perceived in youth work. The report offered new ways of 'valuing' the life experience of volunteers, but at the same time presented a challenge to the professionalisation of work with young people, by suggesting that volunteers might sometimes be more skilled than their so-called 'professional' counterparts. In turn, youth social workers were also looking at how volunteers could strengthen both the community base of the work and the actual practice work.

IT, youth justice, and other similar projects have tended to stress the complementary nature of volunteers' skills. In broad terms, especially in England, the more focused the project is on offending behaviour, the less likely that volunteers will be used for direct contact work with the young people concerned. Youth projects have also varied considerably with regard to which roles volunteers could fulfil. This is still true today. More about this is included later under 'styles' of work.

The rest of this chapter is divided up to offer material exploring some aspects of the following:
- benefits of, and for, volunteers
- recruitment and training
- attitudes
- styles of leadership and work
- support and management
- boundary management

Background

As IT evolved into youth justice and the restorative justice programmes, projects focusing on community safety, safe neighbourhoods, social action and crime prevention co-existed in many localities. Alongside these were general and specialist youth provision, provided by statutory and voluntary agencies and services like after-school clubs and play facilities often provided as an adjunct to education services. In any area, a local audit of service providers will uncover an almost bewildering variety of small and large provisions for young people. In its widest sense, all of these are part of a community crime prevention programme, whether it is a one-night-a-week church-based youth club, scouts and guides, the combined cadets corp, the steel band, majorettes or the junior football teams. What seems to be generally true is that statutory social service and probation services have been less involved with, and committed to, the communities in which they are based.

Because the majority of these will not have been established with any links to social or welfare services, they can easily be overlooked when assessing the contribution of volunteers and members of the community to provision which may help to prevent crime. More obvious are schemes like the Crime Concern Mentoring Programme, through which:

> *Young People, aged 14–21, who have offended or are 'at risk' of offending, are assigned mentors on a one-to-one basis. Mentors comprise a variety of people from all walks of life who volunteer to encourage and advise young people.*   (Crime Concern, 1998)

Another focus of the wider community crime prevention is family and neighbourhood programmes and centres, which may be generally available, or highly focused on specialist need. In many of these schemes parents are involved in ways which give them new skills both for parenting their own children and in some cases in working with other young people. The Kids' Club Network is one of the best known providers of general services through out-of-school clubs, while agencies such as NEWPIN provide befrienders to support mothers who are experiencing stress. In this wider context, Jon Bright wrote in Crime Concern's publication:

> *It should be noted that many of the measures necessary to reduce youth crime are not crime prevention measures. They can have many benefits of which reduced offending is but one. The framework advocated here aims to reduce levels of youth crime by supporting families, enhancing opportunities for young people (especially those at risk) and strengthening neighbourhoods.*   (Bright, 1993)

There are many reasons for targeting parents as beneficiaries of support services. *NACRO* stated that:

> . . . *principal research studies indicate that the factors most significantly related to an increased risk of criminality are:*
> - *economic depression*
> - *poor parental supervision*
> - *parental neglect*
> - *harsh or erratic discipline*
> - *parental conflict*
> - *long-term separation from a biological parent*
> - *having a parent with a criminal record*   (NACRO, 1997)

It is, therefore, proactive to engage in activities which offer parents new skills and confidence for bringing up children. This encourages self-help and may change parents' own perceptions of their abilities. Volunteers are increasingly involved in these parenting skills, in mentoring and befriending schemes, as well as in other aspects of community safety and crime prevention work. The intensity of the work, the skill levels required and the complicating factors of gender, race, age, language and religion can all impact on determining which volunteers are appropriate for particular forms of intervention or preventative scheme.

Benefits of, and for, volunteers

Buried in project reports of hundreds of youth projects and crime prevention initiatives are testimonies to the advantages of using volunteers, and an indication of what they gain from the experience. Here are a few:

Community partnership:

> . . . *The importance of the partnership which exists between the local community and the staff of the Project cannot be underestimated, as it is by far the most important reason for the continued success of our work. This partnership is not a nominal one, but one which exists in all aspects of the life of CYP. Local people make up the bulk of the Management Committee, are heavily involved in all our fund-raising activities and are involved as part of the staff group in all our clubs and activities.*

What volunteers bring to the work:

> *The Project bases its commitment to (volunteers) on several reasons:*
> 1. *Skill sharing: the community contains a large number of resources which can directly benefit the young people in the area.*
> 2. *Volunteers bring a new dimension of adult contact to the young people in groups and clubs.*
> 3. *Involvement leads to local people becoming more aware of our work and actively contributing to the direction of it. We in turn become more accountable to the community.*
> 4. *Involvement in the work of the Project has led to the local community taking a larger responsibility for young people in the area.*
> 5. *Work with families: parental problems are often reflected onto the child and direct involvement with full-time staff has been used to further their personal development.*
>   (Canongate Youth Project, 1986)

Unexpected benefits:
The initial motivation for using volunteers (in group work) was to provide a more wide-ranging and flexible programme. In the event, both their role and the benefits to the programme arising from their greater involvement were much greater than originally envisaged.

They were mostly local people, many had children of their own; and they responded to the young people in a natural manner.

A further unexpected bonus from the involvement of volunteers was the reaction of the young people on learning that the volunteers were working without payment, out of personal choice. The youngsters were impressed . . . The realisation that people do not invariably do things only for money or material gain stimulated the emergence of a much more positive attitude.

(Community Projects Foundation, Swindon Youth Project)

The use of para-professionals has several benefits:
- *Being members of the community, they are able to inter-act both formally and informally with Opstrap parents. They can often communicate with their neighbours more easily than a visiting professional might, and they are in a good position to gain insight into problems facing Opstrap parents.*
- *As no previous experience is necessary to become a para-professional, staffing the Opstrap program with local para-professionals has proved to be not that difficult.*
- *Para-professionals serve as role models for some parents who are seeking a job.*
- *For the para-professionals, the job is often the first step in their career. They learn new skills and gain self-confidence which will help them in the future should they want to look for further employment once their Opstrap job is over.*

(Opstrap Program, Amsterdam from *Social Work in the Netherlands*, 1994)

Stimulation and responsibility:
Our voluntary leaders are a very varied group from graduates to unskilled workers, but many serve a long period of time, the average being five years. We explain this remarkable achievement as follows:
1. *The job itself is stimulating and interesting: people who get involved with a small group enjoy the close relationships that develop with group members.*
2. *The job is a responsible one; the group depends entirely upon the skills and enthusiasm of the voluntary leader.*
3. *The work develops: as members grow older the challenges and style of work changes.*
4. *Considerable personal training and material support is provided by the organisation and recognition is given to problems faced by, and successes of, leaders.*
And industrial management consultant, Frederick Herzberg, has identified the four chief motivators: the work itself; responsibility; opportunity for advancement; and personal growth. Interestingly, working conditions and pay are not included in this list. It is significant that all but opportunity for advancement apply to our voluntary leaders.

(Hart et al. in Adams et al., 1981)

Partnerships:
We not only sought to bring different professional backgrounds together, but also to involve volunteers, students and members of the community, working alongside and with equal status

to social workers, probation officers and teachers. We have consciously not seen volunteers or students as a source of free and cheap labour, to be exploited. Instead, we have recognised the need for a two-way relationship: in return for the service using their existing understanding and skills, we can offer regular support and opportunities for further development. In this way a relationship is developed which is of mutual benefit to the volunteer and the group.

(Harrison, 1982)

Recruitment and training

The *ISTD Handbook of Community Programmes for Young People and Juvenile Offenders* gives the impression that volunteers are still involved in a fair proportion of the staff teams across the diverse range of community initiatives. For instance, the Leeds Victim Offender Unit, which is wholly funded by the Probation Service, describes the staffing as:

Three full-time co-ordinators, one administrator and 16 sessional and volunteer mediators are employed by the unit (they begin as unpaid volunteers and progress to sessional payments when fully trained). All mediators are subject to police checks on their criminal records prior to accreditation as a mediator.   (Martin, 1997)

Recruitment

It seems to us that not much has been written about recruiting volunteers and part-time staff into crime prevention initiatives. It is much more important to attract people who are keen to work with young people, have something they can offer, and are not coming in to 'save' or 'reform' them out of some philanthropic zeal. Equally important is having a screening and interviewing process in place before trying to attract new volunteers. This should include having materials available which explain the focus and aims of the work, the roles of volunteers and information on benefits and commitments. The potential range of jobs and types of involvement is vast.

Here are some suggested ways to recruit volunteers which you may want to consider. This is loosely based on Mark Smith's *Organise!* (1982) and refined by my own experiences.

Word of mouth or personal contact
Often new volunteers are friends or work colleagues of existing full or part-time staff. Personal contact is the easiest and likely to be the most effective method of recruitment. Consider how you can encourage existing staff to be proactive in finding new team members.

Posters and leaflets
A focused campaign using a brief advert asking for staff may attract potential new recruits. Make sure the wording clearly explains what is required and does not appear either too professional or too threatening. Think about the best locations to put up a poster or distribute a flier.

Newspapers and media
A small advert in the local paper, or even better, a short article explaining the aims and nature of the work may bring in some new people. A news item or interview on local radio or access TV can achieve a similar result.

An event
Holding an event can act as a focus for attracting new staff for a project. This may be a stand alone event such as an open-day, or a 'piggy-back' event such as being part of a forum on crime prevention or a planning for real exercise.

Training

With the rise of accreditation for all types of training, there is an increasing use of NVQs and other forms of training which are 'competence' based. Such programmes are dependent upon good supervision and the quality of trainers/assessors. Obviously the training, support and verification procedures of the trainers and assessors are an integral part of the whole package. The nature of the organisation and the profession to which it is allied (e.g. social work, youth work, education, the police) will be a key determinant in defining the shape of the training offered to volunteers.

The learning process is very much on-the-job in most cases. Aspects of such training usually utilise the following aspects:

1. An induction process which explains the aims, philosophy and practice of the work. The person running the induction will usually provide written materials for the trainee, a written contract, and probably introduce a probationary period.
2. In many organisations, the previous experience and skills of the volunteer will be evaluated during the initial training and induction. In NVQ-style training this is often referred to as the 'portfolio' of prior learning.
3. The trainee volunteer is linked to a mentor to 'show them the ropes', introduce them to other staff and users. The volunteer then begins to practice (i.e. learn competences in) the required skills such as group work, counselling or whatever.
4. Assessment of performance depends on the volunteer and the assessor knowing what targets for performance are appropriate. In practice, this might mean being confident and able to run group discussion sessions effectively. And the range of practice may be assessed, for instance, whether they can work with both sexes, different ages, young people of different backgrounds, and understand sexist and other discriminatory practices. Performance criteria in this type of work usually relates to the successful acquisition and understanding of *knowledge* and *skills*.
5. Most training requires the trainee to keep records of performance and practice as well as demonstrating the skills to an assessor. Together, the practice and the written records provide the portfolio of evidence on which the trainee is assessed and accredited.

The following is from Price and Napper. Hopefully, it may provide a framework which can be modified for the organisation of training for volunteers in a youth justice or crime prevention programme. Rather than adopting all of the competences of youth work, it is important to compare them with the needs of the young people you work with, the organisation and the existing staff group. Given that volunteers are offering their time and may have lots of other commitments, it is very important to make sure that the training is as *individually focused and flexibly organised* as possible.

Tim pickles (1987) produced a useful list of core elements at the heart of dealing with team conflicts. These are equally applicable in volunteer development.

What do the competences look like?

In setting the competence statements, the roles, tasks and abilities of a youth worker have been considered in three overlapping areas:

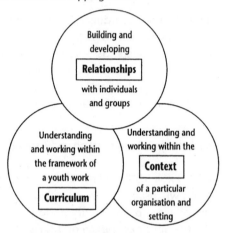

The fifteen *units* of competence which cover these three areas are:

1   *Building on experience*
2   *Building relationships with young people*
3   *Working with groups of young people*
4   *Providing support for young people*   **Relationships**
5   *Confronting bias and discrimination*
6   *Working with other staff*

7   *Planning the youth work curriculum*
8   *Preparing the environment*
9   *Delivering the curriculum*   **Curriculum**
10 *Empowering young people*
11 *Monitoring and evaluating the curriculum*

12 *Working within systems*
13 *Maintaining health and safety*
14 *Acting as an advocate of young people*   **Context**
15 *Working within the community*

Each *unit* of competence is then broken down to a number of *elements*, each with particular *performance criteria* or measures of competence. It is these performance criteria particularly that should be focused on when collecting evidence.

Source: *Competence in Youth Work for Managers and Trainers*, Price and Napper, 1994.

in a modified form, based on tim's list, the aims of development work are:
- To draw out the attitudes, values, and beliefs of team members.
- To identify individual strengths and weaknesses and develop action plans to build on strengths.
- To clarify tasks and roles to be performed by staff members.
- To identify and resolve conflict issues within the staff team.
- To create appropriate and effective support and development structures for individual team members.

Attitudes

The beliefs and attitudes of volunteers are central to how well they will relate to young people and how they will operate within the organisation. Tackling discriminatory attitudes and building positive practices among those who work with young people is vitally important. In the 'real world' nearly everyone will have personal experiences of being discriminatory and being discriminated against. Volunteers should be encouraged to look at their own experiences and to take positive action in their own work with young people to challenge and change discriminatory behaviour from individuals and groups. Bullying and harassment are among the most common forms of discriminatory behaviour.

So what attitudes are youth projects working in this field looking for?

One starting place could be the ethics statement developed by the Fédération Internationale des Communicatives Éducatives for those working with young people:

It is the professional responsibility of everyone to:
- *Value and respect a young person as an individual in their own right, in their role as a member of their family and in their role as a member of the community in which they live.*
- *Respect the relationship of the young person to their parents, their siblings and other members of their family, taking account of their natural ties and interdependent rights and responsibilities.*
- *Enable the normal growth and development of each individual young person to achieve their potential in all aspects of functioning.*
- *Help each young person for whom they bear responsibility by preventing problems where possible, by offering protection where necessary, or by providing care and rehabilitation to counteract or resolve problems faced.*
- *Use information appropriately, respecting the privacy of young people, maintaining confidentiality where necessary and avoiding the misuse of personal information.*
- *Oppose at all times any form of discrimination, oppression or exploitation of young people and preserve their rights.*
- *Maintain personal and professional integrity, develop skills and knowledge in order to work with competence, work co-operatively with colleagues, monitor the quality of services, and contribute to the development of the service and of policy and thinking in the field.*

(FICE n.d.)

It is almost impossible to identify the best attributes for new recruits. Priestley and McGuire (1983) observed that:

Unfortunately, or perhaps fortunately for present purposes, it just does not seem to be the case that good helpers are in any way personally distinct from their less effective counterparts.

However, to engage in groupwork and much other crime prevention work with young people does require an understanding of our self and our attitudes. Some young people may present very real difficulties to particular adults who work with them. This may be because of age, gender, race, sexual preference, physical or mental impairment, and, most obviously, because of offences that the young people have committed. An example sticks in our minds. When a 16-year-old boy raped a girl from a particular youth project based on a housing scheme outside of Edinburgh, there was extreme emotion and disagreement within the staff team as to whether they should continue to work with the boy concerned. Only after a residential staff weekend away from the area did the staff and management of the project reach a somewhat reluctant agreement on how to proceed.

Our attitudes are not fixed in place for ever, and as quite a lot of groupwork and individual work with young people seeks behaviour and attitude change, this is also true through the process of training staff. Along with practice skills, some attributes appropriate for the work are acquired through an experiential process. Volunteers learn a lot from other workers through official or unofficial mentoring. They will also learn through their interactions with young people. There is no list of 'correct' attitudes. The context of each organisation and the nature of the work will play a large part in determining what attitudes and actions are appropriate. For instance, working in an institution such as a prison or school requires a different set of behaviours than in a youth justice group or a youth club.

Again using Priestley and McGuire's work (1983) as a starting point, they suggested that 'those who are good at helping' exhibit the following characteristics:
- Their approach to offering help appears genuine rather than condescending or patronising.
- They show respect for the people they are working with.
- They offer non-judgemental, accepting, warm and empathetic attitudes.
- They are less interested in methods of controlling people.
- They actively show interest in the people they are with.

As an addition to this list, good communication skills both in presenting and listening, seem important. It is fairly obvious that people who have a genuine interest in some of the same activities as young people are likely to make good volunteers. We have personal experience of this in relation to bike and motor projects; music projects and a whole range of sporting activities.

In the National Intermediate Treatment Federation's *Practice Development Papers* (Whitlam, 1981) the Appendix included a contribution from J.M Williams from the University of Birmingham. This concerned the ten skills needed to promote learning in groups. Here it is in a somewhat modified form. It still looks useful as a guide to less experienced staff.

The ten skills
1. Get acquainted. Get to know the other group members, put names to faces and try to remember information about individual members of the group.
2. Learn to co-operate. Help the group to work together, focus on tasks and complete them co-operatively.
3. Recognise the value of all contributions. Individuals should not be ignored, nor should anyone be allowed to monopolise the proceedings.

4. Everyone should be encouraged to contribute. The group should be encouraged to recognise this as a responsibility to the group. Encourage openness and honesty.
5. Respond positively to the contributions of other people. Build on other people's contributions, rather than ignoring them.
6. Develop listening skills and communication skills.
7. Try to perceive areas of difference and of agreement. Encourage group cohesion and agreement.
8. Encourage contributions rather than argument. Group members may tend to discourage other contributions through being too combative. Group members may need to develop ways of responding to each other, and techniques for encouraging more discussion.
9. Learning new roles: help members to try on new roles such as:
   - initiator (introduces new ideas)
   - clarifier (requests further information)
   - summariser (brings group discussion up to date and points out areas of agreement and disagreement)
   - evaluator (points out progress, goals and weaknesses)
10. Arriving at a consensus. Help the group to achieve a truly group agreement; one which is greater than individuals might have achieved. Value individual contributions to the group process.

Styles of leadership and work

Because the range of tasks and styles of work is so vast in this area of work, it is impossible to describe all of them, and therefore we are not even going to try. Instead, we present here some tools for evaluating the types of leadership styles and roles, which, in turn, may assist in allocating tasks, establishing co-worker teams, and generally aiding the individual, the young people involved, and the organisation.

Pickles' Co-working Inventory (see below and next page) is a good place to start. Modify the questions to suit the needs of your organisation and work.

Pickles suggests that the exercise be used in pairs who are likely to be working together. After each person has filled in the inventory, they should share the contents of their inventories with each other, then discuss how they think their responses might affect their ability to work together. Whoever is running the training session should invite the partners to consider:
1. What are your strengths as co-workers?
2. What are your weaknesses as co-workers?
3. What are the possible areas of conflict?
4. What are identifiable gaps in your partnership?
5. Are the differences in your approaches positive or negative?

The following list suggests the variety of roles:
- group workers
- counsellors
- activities co-ordinators
- advocates
- residential workers
- peer tutors
- mentors
- drivers

Co-working inventory

I see myself as the kind of leader who:

makes decisions after consulting others	3 2 1 1 2 3	makes decisions without consulting others
is well organised	3 2 1 1 2 3	is quite chaotic
avoids making decisions	3 2 1 1 2 3	sees a timetable and sticks to it
makes decisions based on information and analysis	3 2 1 1 2 3	makes decisions based on feelings and people's needs and values
is happy to take charge	3 2 1 1 2 3	is happier if someone else takes charge
is able to take criticism	3 2 1 1 2 3	is floored by criticism
is a thinking person	3 2 1 1 2 3	is a feeling person
is comfortable with conflict	3 2 1 1 2 3	is happier when there is consensus
is quiet, thoughtful and prefers time alone	3 2 1 1 2 3	is active, energetic and prefers time with other people
helps others explore their feelings	3 2 1 1 2 3	helps others to make logical decisions
is happier with definite plans	3 2 1 1 2 3	is happy to leave things vague
likes logical people	3 2 1 1 2 3	likes emotional people
is stubborn when thwarted	3 2 1 1 2 3	is easy going
likes change and keeping options open	3 2 1 1 2 3	likes predictability and knowing in advance
is manipulative	3 2 1 1 2 3	works in an open way
communicates little of my inner thoughts and feelings	3 2 1 1 2 3	communicates freely my inner thoughts and feelings
records groups, interviews etc as fully as possible	3 2 1 1 2 3	keeps minimal recordings on groups, interviews etc.
is popularity seeking	3 2 1 1 2 3	copes easily with being unpopular
needs clarity	3 2 1 1 2 3	can tolerate ambiguity
is able to reveal self freely	3 2 1 1 2 3	is reserved about revealing self
feels comfortable with physical contact	3 2 1 1 2 3	shies away from physical contact
feels uncomfortable when seen to be wrong	3 2 1 1 2 3	is able to cope with being publicly seen to be wrong
likes being the centre of attention	3 2 1 1 2 3	is reserved
is inclined to busy myself in doing things	3 2 1 1 2 3	is likely to take time to stop and chat with people

(Pickles, 1987)

- outreach workers
- specialist workers on drugs (or other) issues
- befrienders
- outdoors or environmental workers

- catering
- domiciliary
- managers
- community advisors

Add your own to the list.

Here are two exercises from *Worth the Risk?* (Ball, 1987) which can be useful to develop discussion about styles of work with young people.

Exercise 1

This exercise is an attempt to explore the personal philosophies of workshop participants, in relation to groupwork with offenders:

(a) Read the questionnaire.

(b) Working individually, tick the statement nearest to your own attitude; work through all the paired statements from 1 to 14.

(c) Score your responses for each statement. Add scores, and determine both your total score and ranking.

(d) Pair off respective highest and lowest scores until all participants are paired off. Wherever possible pair off participants with different rankings.

(e) Undertake short *two-way* interviews to determine each person's 'philosophy' or attitude towards work with offenders. Specifically:

- Identify what you believe to be Agency policy on the purpose of groupwork.
- Explain your views on offenders' levels of culpability and responsibility.
- Explain what you are trying to achieve in groupwork, or describe your personal style.

(f) Each pair to feedback differences between individuals' responses, to the large group.

Questionnaire

When running a group, I prefer to:

1a. Share my perceptions with young people.

1b. Tell young people what's 'right' and 'wrong'.

2a. Treat group members as children.

2b. Treat group members as adults.

3a. Be humorous whenever possible.

3b. Be strict whenever possible.

4a. Relate to young people on their cultural level.

4b. Relate as a wiser adult.

5a. Be open and accepting of young peoples' values wherever possible.

5b. Be critical of young people's values wherever possible.

6a. Confront young people regularly.

6b. Be 'non threatening'.

7a. Put young people at ease wherever possible.

7b. Put young people under pressure wherever possible.

8a. Be relaxed.

8b. Be guarded.

9a. Take risks in a session.

9b. Run a 'tight ship' in a session.

10a. Be directive.

10b. Be non-directive.

11a. Share personal information about myself.   11b. Give no personal information.
12a. Avoid difficult subjects.   12b. Discuss difficult subjects.
13a. Encourage freedom of group members to   13b. Change young people's
    make decisions.   behaviour.
14a. Form strong opinions about young people   14b. Form no strong opinions about
    in the group.   anyone.

Scoring

The questionnaire statements are obviously somewhat extreme and reflect either end of a continuum between controlling and non-controlling in terms of groupwork practice. Responses to each pairing are therefore bound to be somewhat generalised, but marking your response in terms of the statement nearest to your own attitude when describing your overall groupwork style, should show up any significant differences between staff members.

		Total Score	Rankings
1a. 4.	1b. 1.		
2a. 1.	2b. 4.		
3a. 4.	3b. 1.	14–26 points	Rank A
4a. 4.	4b. 1.	27–36 points	Rank B
5a. 4.	5b. 1.	37–46 points	Rank C
6a. 1.	6b. 4.	47–56 points	Rank D
7a. 4.	7b. 1.		
8a. 4.	8b. 1.		
9a. 4.	9b. 1.		
10a. 1.	10b. 4.		
11a. 4.	11b. 1.		
12a. 1.	12b. 4.		
13a. 4.	13b. 1.		
14a. 1.	14b. 4.		

Exercise 2

Tolerance levels of workers (Controlling/Non-controlling continuum)

This exercise offers a practical way for a team to explore leadership issues in more detail. The focus is largely on 'tolerance levels', but also raises issues of style, purpose of groupwork and co-working.

1. Where do you think each team member would place themselves on this continuum?
    Controlling . . . . Non-controlling
2. List five words which best describe your style of groupwork with young people.
3. What is your worst quality in groupwork with young people?
4. List three things you would not tolerate from young people.
5. List five words which best describe your style of interaction with other groupworkers.
6. What is your worst quality in your work with colleagues?

7. List three things you would not tolerate from colleagues.
8. List three to five words to describe what you expect from other groupworkers.

If you wish to explore team issues about philosophy in more depth, tackle these extra items:
a. List three to five anxieties or fears you have about your work with (i) young people (ii) other staff.
b. Identify specific rules your group has agreed.
c. Identify explicit rules that have arisen.
d. Make a one-sentence statement on the ethos of the group as you see it.
e. Reach a team consensus on the ethos of the group.
f. Reach a consensus on the expectations of the young people in the group.

As a final comment, we felt it might be illuminating to share the variety of responses workshop participants gave to Section e of the first exercise. These illustrate the range of possible responses, even within a broad consensus, about the purpose of groupwork with young offenders:

1. Identify what you believe to be agency policy on the purpose of groupwork:
- Reducing offending
- Keeping young people out of custody
- Looking at offending patterns
- Diverting from crime
- Changing behaviour
- Challenging perceptions
- Making young people aware of the implications of offending

2. Explain your views on offenders' levels of culpability and responsibility:
- Young people don't understand the consequences of their actions
- There are age-related mitigating factors
- Young people have limited perceptions
- Young people are often labelled
- Young people are responsible to a degree
- Environmental factors have an enormous influence
- Difficult to define; lack of parental care?

3. Explain what you are trying to achieve in groupwork:
- Providing an alternative to custody
- Using the group as a self-help focus for work
- Helping young people to gain a clearer understanding of themselves
- Helping young people to make their own decisions
- Self assessment and awareness
- Developing self esteem
- Offering choices
- Stopping offending
- Bringing out the positive parts of young people

- Achieving personal growth
- Encouraging young people to stop or reduce offending

4. . . . or describe your personal style:
- Helper and facilitator
- Informative style
- Humourous and confrontational
- Trying to be equal
- Honesty, humorous and relaxed
- Aware of cultural issues
- Subtle manipulator
- Flexible approach
- Non-judgemental
- Openness and honesty
- Encouragement
- Being a mum   (Ball, 1987)

It may also be useful to re-visit the table derived by Thorpe et al. from their groundbreaking study *Out of Care: The Community Support of Juvenile Offenders* (1980). This model of community support and involvement in work with juveniles is based on different intensities of work with young people. Interestingly, volunteers were seen as being valuable at all four levels of intensity.

Support and management

Volunteers require careful nurturing. Many projects working with young people involved in criminal behaviour could not exist without volunteers. As we have already indicated, volunteers may manage a project, staff it and provide ancillary services, including the all-important fund-raising. Management and support of youth crime prevention (and similar) projects is a very mixed affair. Many projects are time limited; funding comes from an enormous variety of sources; statutory and/or voluntary organisations may be involved in management; evaluation and monitoring can be done internally or by external consultants and agencies. Rather than try to unpick all the permutations of organisational structure, the following offers some models and insights into management and support considerations and issues which can help meet the personal and development needs of volunteers and ultimately benefit the service provision and the consumers of that service.

Doug Nicholls (1995) wrote in relation to model job descriptions:

> All too often part-time staff are shoved into a post with no induction, no training and no clear statement of expected role. The job description is an essential requirement . . . One of the main causes of stress in youth and community work is a lack of clarity about role and mixed messages of expectation. A good job description and contract coupled with regular supervision can significantly contribute to a good working environment free from stress and full of reward.

The organisation of community support for juvenile offenders

Facility	Programme	Staffing	Client	Disposal
High intensity day care (some weekend work).	Correctional curriculum. Vocational training. Remedial education. Leisure activities.	Intermediate treatment centre social workers. Remedial teachers. Trade instructors. Volunteers.	High-risk persistent offender (decarcerated or diverted from custody). Unable to attend school or work.	To evening care or weekly group.
High-intensity evening care (some weekend work).	Correctional curriculum. Vocational training and remedial education if necessary. Leisure activities.	Intermediate treatment centre social workers. Remedial teachers and trade instructors, if necessary. Volunteers.	High-risk persistent offender (decarcerated or diverted from custody). Attending school or working.	To weekly group or youth club.
Medium-intensity weekly group (perhaps some weekend work).	Modified correctional curriculum. Leisure activities.	Area intermediate treatment social worker. Other social workers/youth workers. Volunteers.	Persistent petty offender, at risk of further offending.	To youth club or other positive leisure activity.
Low-intensity (youth club or other structured leisure activity).	Leisure activities.	Youth workers. Volunteers.	Occasional offender.	Continuing attendance without official direction.

(Thorpe et al., 1980)

The main functions of a job description are to:
- *Outline the main duties and responsibilities.*
- *Establish lines of accountability and communication.*
- *Clarify expectations.*
- *Provide a baseline for assessing performance and work.*
- *Set parameters.*
- *Focus work in times of conflicting demands.*   (Nicholls, 1995)

One of the books we always referred to when looking at support structures for staff, especially those working at the margins and in vulnerable situations, was *The Management of Detached Work* by Alan Rogers and colleagues (1981). Although focused on detached and outreach work, many aspects of the book have relevance to any type of youth project. Below we offer one section from that publication on establishing a management committee and its constitution. As Doug Nicholls pointed out above, management is often haphazard and support is non-existent. This is a major contributory factor to the burn-out rate and frustration which frequently occurs. Just as young people need to know their boundaries, part-time and voluntary staff need clear guidance on what their job is and how they are expected to perform it.

Constitution and formulation of the management committee

If the project is to be (or be part of) a voluntary organisation with charitable status it will need a written constitution acceptable to the Charity Commission. The timing of establishing the constitution is very important.

It is easier for a group that is still forming and constituting itself to register as a charity than one that is established. Therefore, if you decide that it would be to your group's advantage to have charitable status later on, you should consider registering as a charity while you are establishing your constitution.

It is important that in the first instance you send your draft constitution, before you formally adopt it, to the Charity Commission for their comment. If you are located in Scotland or Northern Ireland, the Charity Division of the Inland Revenue rather than the Charity Commission will give you this advice. Only after it has been agreed by the relevant authority that your organisation would be charitable should you adopt your constitution.

If, however, you have to establish your organisation before Charity Commission approval has been obtained, make sure that your constitution expressly allows any amendment to be made for the purposes of achieving charitable status.

The structure of the constitution should follow this outline:
1. The name of the organisation or project.
2. The objectives and aims of the particular detached work project.
3. The membership of the committee and the rights and duties.
4. The number of meetings held, including the annual general meeting of the project and voting rights.
5. The functions and powers of the committee.

---

6. The control of finance.
7. The rules and procedures at all meetings, and the dissolution of the committee.
8. Any alterations to the constitution.

More information can be obtained from the Charity Commission about drawing up a constitution; though this is a time for getting advice from someone experienced, such as a solicitor, in drawing up such a document. Books and guides will be useful and it would be helpful to obtain a copy of a constitution from an existing detached work project if that is possible.

Representation on a management committee could come from the following groups:
1. Local authority departments, including councillors.
2. Government agencies and funding bodies.
3. Tenants associations.
4. Community or action groups.
5. Local tradesmen.
6. Trade unions, chamber of commerce, industry.
7. Solicitors, lawyers, etc.
8. Voluntary organisations, churches.
9. Education establishments.
10. Young People within the community.
11. Others which relate to local circumstances (maybe the existing steering group).

The value to a detached work project of a strong constituted management committee with the right kind of people and agencies represented on it, will be to establish credibility between the project and other agencies, the community and young people. This will enhance the status of the work: youth work and young people generally tend to be given a low priority by the majority of the adult population.

When the management committee is constituted the broad responsibilities of the committee will be:
1. Obtaining finance and resources for the project.
2. Appointing staff.
3. Accountability to funders and the Charity Commission.
4. Managing, supporting and monitoring the work of the project.   (Rogers et al., 1981)

From experience of project management it seems important to clarify the relationship between volunteers and part-time staff and:
- funding bodies
- the employing organisation
- the management, steering group or advisory committee
- full-time staff
- management committee and staff team meetings
- any supervisors used by the organisation
- other organisations or community groups
- users

Some organisations use 'key' or 'link' workers to offer one-to-one supervision and support for volunteer staff. This supervision usually entails regular meetings and may or may not be part of the accountability process and management supervision. Given that much of the work may also take place in groups or in situations where staff are paired up, volunteers may also find themselves working with a 'co-worker'. It is likely because of their inter-dependence that they will develop a strong relationship and use each other for support.

Volunteer and part-time staff also need personal supervision to ensure that their own personal development and training needs are catered for. And, on occasions, like any other staff, they may need a shoulder to cry on, or a person to groan and moan to. This sort of support is best kept separate from the accountability structure, though if the volunteer wishes to relay some of the information back to the managers, this is obviously permissible. Through this sort of structure it should be possible to deal with:

- practical matters
- confidential and personal concerns
- management issues and conflicts
- training and staff development

Warren Feek's (1982) useful model for a supervision and performance appraisal follows:

Supervision and performance appraisal

These are words that scare people! They have a number of meanings, attract many myths and have encouraged considerable debate. Essentially the accent is on supporting each team member within the overall framework of the agency.

The importance of this is that if the components of a team are not functioning well, the team will be weak. Not all members of a team have the same needs or strengths so each must be looked at individually.

Two of the big debates in this area are: first: should supervision and appraisal be informal or formal? The approach below assumes that it will be formal in that a set time and place will have been arranged for the session and an agreed structure for the session will be followed.

That hints at the second question: who should be involved in the supervision and appraisal sessions? Should the staff person you are responsible to conduct them? Would an outsider with knowledge of the field be better? Can supervision and appraisal by peers work? Is it possible to conduct them as a staff group? These are debates for your agency to conduct and resolve. Irrespective of the answer arrived at and the format adopted, the following areas should be covered:

Supervision is a regular (monthly) look at the tasks being performed:
- Take the task headings of the job description in turn.
- What work is being done in each section?
- What particular areas are giving difficulty? How can the problems be resolved?
- What work went well? Why?
- Is the work done matching the job definition?

- Are there any problems of relationships with other members of the team which need looking at now (i.e. too important to wait for the appraisal)?
- Are there any training needs which should be dealt with now?
- What action has been taken on the training programme agreed at the last appraisal?

Appraisal is a biennial assessment of the worker's skills. Whereas supervision concentrates on the task section of the job description, appraisal concentrates on the skills section. To some extent the following should happen:
- The skills needed in the job must be identified. For this exercise a more comprehensive list than is in the job description may be necessary.
- A system for gauging performance should be decided. Possibilities are a scale of letters (A = excellent) or a written descriptive comment, or a verbal summary with written notes indicating action to take place.
- The areas of weakness which it is agreed to work on should be identified.
- Future aims should be agreed.   (Feek, 1982)

Boundary management

Through my own personal contact with Eastern Raven's Trust in Stockton we were aware of the work that their early leader, Alistair Lindsay put into developing the concept of boundary management. The material below comes from the Eastern Raven's Trust report in A Measure of Diversion (1981) by Adams et al. This describes a very particular use of boundaries, but thinking through their use can help provide both young people and staff with a coherent structure for the work.

Boundary management

To demonstrate the need for boundaries, let us consider a family on whom we used to call at 8.30 am to help the seven children, all chronic truants aged between six and 13, to get to school. The children would creep one by one into the living room. One would open the cupboard to be enveloped in an avalanche of clothes. Each child might find his clothes. They might be clean. The food cupboard might be empty. At school the child might be late and might get the cane. At lunch time Mam might be at home, and so on. Each **might** represents a missing boundary. Eastern Ravens' job is, on group nights, to replace these **mights** by **wills**, not in the compulsory sense but in the predictable sense. For example: '. . . you will be accepted as a member of this group . . .' '. . . the group **will** meet every Wednesday . . .' '. . . however naughty you are, you **will** always be welcome . . .'

The needs of these children had been met only partially. For them to grow emotionally and achieve a sense of identity, unpredictability needed to be replaced by predictability, failure by success, confusion by clarity, and inconsistent by consistent treatment. Group leaders see members for only a few hours each week, mainly at group meetings. It is therefore vital to take every opportunity to identify, create and maintain certain critical boundaries around the life of the group.

Forming and operating the group

As a new group is formed, a number of decisions have to be made: about the sex of the group members; about the size of the group – never more than eight; about the ages of the children – never more than 12 years old, with no more than a two year span. Group members are drawn from an area with a concentration of problem families and we ensure that the group members live within about 200 yards of each other. Since families know each other very well, the community becomes sympathetic to Eastern Ravens and supportive of resulting behaviour and life style changes among group members. This is necessary to avoid alienation or reversion and our experience is that we successfully avoid both. These decisions provide a number of boundaries between the group and its environment; they are quite clear and reduce to a manageable level the number of dynamics within the group.

To give the youngsters the opportunity to grow emotionally, it is necessary to erect a structure around the group in operation and maintain it pretty rigidly, helping the children first to adapt to it, then to grow within it. The structure consists of seven key boundaries, five of which are easy to apply, while two require a high degree of social skill.

Membership boundary
Once members have joined, group membership is kept constant. Compare the fixed group with the home where there is a continual change of family as relatives or neighbours or even Mam move in and out.

Leadership boundary
The leaders work only with their own group. This avoids the question, 'is he really interested in us or does he like them more?'

End-point boundary
This boundary is important because it does not exist. The group continues for as many years as members want it to. We try to make sure that there are no grounds for anxiety about rejection from the group.

The emotional significance of these three boundaries to the members, through their experience of the group, becomes: 'This is our group; they are our leaders; and we do belong to this group. We have tested the leaders and we know that they won't reject us'. These are all fundamental emotional needs satisfied by simple boundary management.

Time boundaries
By ensuring that the group meets at the same time on the same evening of each week, a regular, predictable and enjoyable influence is introduced into the lives of the members. This contrasts with the lack of such influences in their home environment, resulting from their inability to capture a sense of time or fit in with others.

Space boundaries
It is important that the group is clear what space it has at its disposal. We achieve this in two ways: with a small clubhouse where one group on its own will use the whole building, and with a minibus. Compare clear space boundaries with some members' homes, where

they often do not know which bedroom, or bed, they will sleep in. They cannot look after their own clothes or toys because others in the family do not accept individual ownership of space. The Land Rover, late at night, gives rise to feelings of warmth and security triggering some very significant discussions. Space boundaries in that situation are crystal clear.

The remaining two boundaries require a lot of sensitivity and skill to apply.

Behavioural boundaries
Deeply ingrained in our group members is a dislike and a resentment of rules. There are probably only three rules of any real importance:
- Don't put yourself or anyone else in danger.
- Don't damage property.
- Don't damage the relationship between the group and the outside world, for example damaging the fence belonging to the farmer on whose land you are camping.

Any rules over and above these are likely to hinder emotional growth, and there are many rules which should be avoided, especially those designed to meet the needs of the leaders rather than the members, such as no running, no shouting, and no boots. However, when one of the basic groundrules is broken, this must not be ignored, but should be responded to in some appropriate way. As a result of this consistency, the member will be helped to recognise the importance of these rules.

Relationship boundaries
Emotional growth is maximised by establishing as close a relationship as possible between leader and member. This is limited by the extent to which the leader can accept the member's behaviour. The relationship is less close if a leader finds his eating habit distasteful, or if he believes it is in some way wrong for members of his group to visit his own home, or regards it as right to know group members' incomes but wrong for them to know his.

(Adams et al., 1981)

In summary

We have brought together a lot of material about using, and not abusing volunteers, because in community partnerships in community safety their role will probably prove crucial. Many statutory agencies have failed to realise the potential of such partnership working. Perhaps some of the material we have collected in this section will help to redress the balance, and return volunteers to the central position they once occupied on the frontline of work with young people in trouble.

References

(Because the project reports quoted early in this section are out of print, we have restricted this list to published books and national reports).
Ball, K. et al. (1987) *Worth the Risk? Creative Groupwork with Young Offenders.* SCF/West Yorkshire Probation Service.
Booton, F. (1985) *Studies in Social Education.* Benfield Press.
Bright, J. (1993) *Youth Crime Prevention: A Framework for Local Action.* Crime Concern.

Butters, S. (1984) *Starting from Strengths*. National Youth Bureau.

Canongate Youth Project (1986) *Developing an Integrated Approach*. CYP.

Crime Concern Mentoring Programme (1998) *Partners in Community Safety*. Crime Concern.

Feek, W. (1982) *The Way We Work*. National Youth Bureau.

FICE (n.d.) *Code of Ethics for Working with Young People*. FICE.

Harrison, M. (1982) *Give 'em a Break*. National Youth Bureau.

Hart, V., Lindsay, A. and Lindsay, K. Eastern Raven's Trust in Adams, R. et al. (1981) *A Measure of Diversion*. National Youth Bureau.

Hesser, K-N. and Koole, W. (1994) *Social Work in the Netherlands*. SWP Publishing, Utrecht.

Martin, C. (1997) *The ISTD Handbook of Community Programmes for Young and Juvenile Offenders*. ISTD/Waterside.

NACRO Young Offenders' Committee (1997) *A New Three Rs for Young Offenders*. NACRO.

Nicholls, D. (1995) *Employment Practice and Policies in Youth and Community Work*. Russell House Publishing.

Pickles, T. (1987) *Working with Young People in Trouble: A Practical Manual*. Intermediate Treatment Resource Centre.

Price, M. and Napper, R. (1994) *Competence in Youth Work for Managers and Trainers*. Longman.

Priestley, P. and McGuire, J. (1983) *Learning to Help: Basic Skills Exercises*. Tavistock.

Rogers, A. et al. (1981) *The Management of Detached Work*. NAYC.

Smith, M. (1982) *Organise!* National Association of Youth Clubs.

Thorpe, D. et al. (1980) *Out of Care: The Community Support of Young Offenders*. Allen and Unwin.

Whitlam, M. (Ed.) (1981) *Practice Development Papers*. NITF.

CHAPTER 9

Working with the victims of young offenders: what works?

Brian Williams

Introduction

Becoming a victim of crime can be a difficult experience, and for some people the experience of dealing with the criminal justice system makes matters even worse. In societies that concentrate attention on punishing offenders, the victim can feel excluded. There are alternatives to this *retributive* approach, however. Victims can be much more involved, and many of them find this process helpful. This *restorative* approach is common in some societies, and efforts have recently been made to adapt it for use in other countries. It involves creating opportunities (and obligations) which allow offenders to make good the damage they have done to the victim.

Although some youth justice workers in England and Wales have considerable experience of working with victims of crime, it is only since the implementation of the Crime and Disorder Act 1998 that such work has become commonplace. Consequently, there is little research evidence about the most effective ways to engage with the victims of young offenders in this country. Some of what is known about work with adult offenders may be relevant, but work with victims in that area has not attracted much research interest either: funding agencies have not seen such enquiries as a high priority.

Restorative approaches to criminal justice acknowledge that not all victims will welcome direct approaches from 'their' offenders. The offence may still be fresh in their minds, and they may be too hurt or angry to contemplate direct contact with the offender. However, reparation allows a range of restorative actions by offenders, from direct apologies and actual repairs to damaged property, to unpaid work that symbolises their regret and puts something back into the wider community.

The pilot projects (late 1998 to spring 2000) for reparation orders in England and Wales were thoroughly evaluated, and the interim report of this research provides some useful pointers for future practice. Research was conducted by Jim Dignan of Sheffield University, and the results formally published in summary form in February 2000 (Dignan, 2000). The Home Secretary has yet to publish the final report. The Thames Valley Police experiment with restorative cautioning has also generated some very interesting research findings. Again, no final publication has yet emerged, although Thames Valley Police have received a confidential report, and the researchers have published some of their preliminary findings (Young and Goold, 1999; Young, 2000). Work with victims has become highly controversial, and it is central to the government's youth justice reforms. As such, it is politically sensitive, and so is research into its effectiveness.

In this chapter, I will draw upon the early experience of youth offending teams (YOTs) (some of whose work I am involved in evaluating), and on the published research from this country and abroad, to make some tentative statements about effective practice. It is important to note, though, that little is known with any degree of certainty about good practice in working with the victims of young offenders. Reparation orders and the other reparative interventions set up by the 1998 Act represent a massive experiment, and although research is in hand, it will be some time before there is reliable information about the effectiveness of the new disposals.

Experience in other countries

There is, however, a longer tradition of work with victims in other countries, and some of this work has been the subject of evaluative research. Without attempting to summarise it all, this section briefly describes some practice and research findings from a number of other countries.

The use of **family group conferences** to deal with young offenders in Australasia has captured the imagination of many youth justice workers in other countries, and there is good evidence of its effectiveness (Morris and Maxwell, 2000). Sadly, the findings of this research have not always been borne in mind when attempting to transfer the family group conferencing approach to other criminal justice systems.

Family group conferences are arranged by an independent facilitator who prepares the participants for the meeting and makes the practical arrangements. Meetings normally involve the victim of the offence and someone who attends to support them. Sometimes they are also accompanied by family members and other people affected less directly by the offence. The offender also comes with family or other supporters, and may also wish to involve professional people such as a social worker, or respected acquaintances such as sports coaches, teachers or neighbours. The meeting aims to agree a resolution of the problems caused by the offence, usually involving some form of reparation by the offender which is satisfactory to all concerned.

The key idea behind family group conferences is John Braithwaite's notion of 'reintegrative shaming' (Braithwaite, 1989). By this he means creating an opportunity for a young offender to face the consequences of their offending and also make reparation to the victim, with both parties supported through the decision-making process. The unacceptability of the offending behaviour is highlighted, but this is immediately followed by a discussion of reparation, and as such the *shaming* of the young person occurs *within a context of reintegration*. Family group conferences replace youth courts almost altogether in Australia and New Zealand, and this builds on a tradition of restorative approaches in Maori communities which pre-dated the court system and academic formulae such as Braithwaite's. The possibility of a court hearing is held in reserve for very serious cases, but a restorative system has effectively replaced the previous retributive one. This involves a philosophical leap which the criminal justice system in England and Wales has yet to make. Rather than treating crime as an offence against the state, it is seen as harm to a victim which can normally be remedied through dialogue between victim and offender, with community support (Fattah, 1998).

Family group conferences have been markedly successful by any standards. In New Zealand they led to a reduction in the population of young people in institutional care of 80 per cent in the decade following their introduction, and conferences succeeded in resolving issues to the satisfaction of both parties in a majority of criminal cases (Muncie, 1999). Although there were difficulties with the conferencing system at first, these appear to have been satisfactorily resolved in New Zealand, with less evidence in recent years of the problems initially experienced when trying to involve victims fully in the process (Morris and Maxwell, 2000).

Politicians and senior police officers in this country have 'cherry-picked' the aspects of family group conferencing which appeal to their sense of justice or which they feel have popular appeal. For example, they have seized on the notion of 'naming and shaming' without seeing the crucial significance of placing shaming in the context of reintegration. In the process, they are in danger of losing the essence of the idea of family group conferences, namely the concept of reintegrative shaming and the model of empowering young offenders, their families and their victims by allowing them to make the decisions. Instead, a watered-down version of the conferences is being used as a replacement for cautioning in some areas, while something much more like a family group conference has been developed in other areas as a vehicle for delivering the new reparation orders (see below).

Experiments with **mediation between offenders and the victims of serious offences** (including, in some cases, mediation between offenders and the surviving relatives of murder victims) show that restorative justice can be applied in very serious cases. In Canada and the USA, recently developed projects have demonstrated that victims are willing to meet incarcerated young offenders responsible for very violent offences, and that both parties can benefit from such mediation if it is properly facilitated (Umbreit et al., 1999). However, such work is at an early stage, and the authors warn against unduly enthusiastic attempts at replicating it elsewhere:

> *There have already been numerous examples of well intentioned criminal justice officials and individual mediators who are too quick to refer or facilitate the use of mediation and dialogue in crimes of severe violence without having first secured advanced training and mentoring. Many unintended negative consequences could result from such initiatives, including a significant re-victimisation of the victim.*   (Umbreit et al., 1999)

These experiments need to be properly evaluated, and their direct relevance to other criminal justice systems cannot be taken for granted. Nevertheless, they call into question the common assumption that restorative justice is mainly applicable to minor offending. The families of North American murder victims were anxious to meet the offenders, not least because they were the last to see the victim alive. Families and offenders alike sought closure and 'healing'. The offenders often hoped for forgiveness: mediation created a safe environment in which surviving family members could explain why this was not possible for them, but also allowed them to express their belief that the young offender could change.

More limited, and still experimental, arrangements for **victim-offender mediation** as an alternative or complementary approach to a generally retributive criminal justice system exist in a number of countries. In Italy, the outcome of mediation is reported to the magistrate and may lead to the case being dropped (Gatti and Ceretti, 1998). In Sweden, there is a network of local mediation projects, and victim-offender mediation is considered appropriate in the case of violent as well as property offences. However, a properly evaluated experiment which may lead to the introduction of a formal disposal of mediation is a recent development there (Lindstrom and Svanberg, 1998). Similar experiments are taking place in Germany, Switzerland, Belgium, Norway, Finland and Sweden. In a number of other countries, mediation is allied to unpaid community service, and the young person can compensate the victim or undertake such work after mediation takes place, for example in Austria and Spain (Schelkens, 1998; Justice, 2000).

In Northern Ireland, pilot community restorative justice projects in a number of areas aim to replace paramilitary punishments with victim-offender mediation. These are to be independently evaluated. This is an important development, on the one hand as part of the peace process, and also because it represents an attempt to replace both the former state monopoly on criminal justice and the parallel paramilitary structures with community-sanctioned alternatives (McEvoy and Gormally, 2000). Mediators have succeeded in reintegrating some young offenders into their original communities, despite the tradition of forcible exile previously used to deal with persistent recidivists. Punishment beatings and shootings have, however, continued alongside these community mediation initiatives.

Experience in the pilot youth offending teams

A number of important lessons emerged from the experience of the areas which piloted the new inter-agency youth offending teams in England and Wales during the period 1998-2000. It became clear that adequate staff training was particularly important where work with victims was concerned, and that such training tended to raise complex questions about ways of protecting confidentiality and the need for intensive preparation before attempting reparative interventions. Concerns about the confidentiality of information provided by victims are likely to be heightened when the Human Rights Act 1998 comes into force in October 2000. Offenders will then probably have a right to access to such information (Crawford and Enterkin, forthcoming). This, in turn, raised questions about whether courts would be willing to adjourn cases for long enough to allow adequate preparatory work with both victims and offenders to take place (Dignan, 1999, 2000; Williams, 2000). The need for such preparation clashes in practice with the government's policy of rewarding courts for 'fast tracking' and dealing with cases more quickly (Williams, 1999). This conflict needs discussion at a local level, with a view to convincing courts of the merits of adjourning cases for full assessments of the potential for reparation.

Although many youth justice workers were initially reluctant to become involved in working with victims, the YOTs which invested time and resources in victim awareness training seem to have reaped some benefits. Some staff who initially expressed resistance to direct work with victims on principled grounds, later came to find it rewarding and ethically justifiable. This was a similar pattern to the earlier experience in the probation service (Williams, 1999a).

Dignan's research on the experimental projects implementing reparation orders found that victims in the pilot areas were not always consulted, in practice, before courts ordered reparative interventions. This clearly contradicts the intentions of the legislation, and the National Standards for Youth Justice (YJB, 2000), setting out official expectations of youth justice workers, were accordingly tightened up to make it clear that such abuses are unacceptable, clearly stating that:

> . . . the wishes of victims in relation to their involvement in restorative justice processes should be respected by YOT staff at all times.   (YJB, 2000)

Local youth offending teams have found it useful to negotiate with benches about the circumstances in which reparation is most appropriate. Magistrates and clerks need to be prepared for their new powers, and ideally they should understand the principles underlying restorative approaches. They will then be more likely to give reparative interventions the necessary time, and to order them in appropriate cases.

While some youth offending teams assumed that their police officer members were best equipped to plan and undertake victim contact work, others came to realise that the need to involve victim support agencies in the planning of this work required other staff to liaise with them. Relationships between such groups and the police were strained in some areas, because the work of racial harassment, rape crisis and women's aid groups inevitably involves public criticism of the police (Williams, 1999b). The involvement of such groups can be beneficial, however, and it broadens the range of approaches open to teams: the probation service, in its victim contact work, tended to over-rely on one voluntary agency, Victim Support. In some areas, existing mediation schemes were willing to take on some of the direct work with young offenders, at least initially (Dignan, 2000).

Experience since June 2000

Youth offending teams have developed a variety of ways of working with the victims of young offenders, and practice has been influenced by a wide range of theoretical models.

In the case of **restorative cautioning**, the Thames Valley Police restorative conferencing approach has been extremely influential in the development of youth offending teams' approaches to final warnings. Essentially, restorative conferencing involves introducing victim concerns into decision-making about relatively minor offences. Victims are sometimes directly involved in the meetings at which final warnings (and previously formal cautions) are delivered. Where victims cannot, or do not wish to be present, police officers sometimes speak on their behalf (Young and Goold, 1999). In the Thames Valley, this system has operated since 1998 after a pilot scheme in one part of the area in 1994, and recently its staff have provided free training sessions for youth justice workers in other areas, spreading the Thames Valley model across the country. Restorative conferences in this model are police-led rather than employing independent co-ordinators to balance the interests of the various parties, as in those areas which have modelled their practice more closely upon family group conferences. This approach has some disadvantages.

Family group conferences are 'underpinned by notions of family empowerment', whereas restorative conferences are primarily designed to meet the priorities of the police (Jackson, 1999). Once the principle of independent facilitation is discarded, the rehabilitative aims of conferencing can quickly get lost. This can lead to net-widening, because there is no independent check on the seriousness of the cases brought before conferences (Justice, 2000). The original aims of the process tend to become obscured, as facilitators increasingly pursue their own agendas rather than concentrating upon the needs of the victims and young offenders taking part in the conferences. There is some evidence that the Thames Valley model has fallen prey to this kind of 'mission drift', and that it therefore fails to meet the prerequisites of effective practice (Young and Goold, 1999). It is not appropriately targeted: indeed, it concentrates its resources on the lowest risk group of young offenders. It does not necessarily lead to appropriate follow-up with individual young people, and it does not target the type of needs which lead young people to commit crime (as its own publicity material admits). The assumption seems to be that a process which is satisfying for many participants is a good thing in itself: but the history of juvenile justice is littered with examples of such good intentions leading to harmful, unintended consequences for young offenders (Haines and Drakeford, 1998; Williams, 2000).

However, **family group conferences** (FGCs) have been successfully introduced in a number of areas for more serious young offenders. In some places, experiments were already in progress before the introduction of the 1998 Crime and Disorder Act. Like the other new reparative interventions, these are being evaluated both by local and national research teams. Some areas have renamed FGCs to distinguish them more clearly from restorative conferences. In several youth offending teams, for example, they are known as Family Group Meetings (which also reflects the fact that they were so called when they were first used with non-offending young people to make decisions about local authority care).

The conference or meeting is seen as a serious intervention in the lives of young offenders and their victims, demanding considerable resources, and it is generally reserved for more serious cases. Independent facilitators are used, and some youth offending teams have contracted with voluntary mediation services or other outside agencies to employ, train and supervise these workers.

The voluntary nature of participation by all parties is emphasised, and consequently there has been considerable resistance to making such meetings formal conditions of court orders. In most areas, this has been successfully negotiated with youth courts, which have a range of other, legally enforceable, orders available to them when required.

Although it was initially expected that **reparation orders** would come into force in April 2000, their introduction was postponed until June and in practice, not all youth offending teams were in a position to implement the new orders immediately then. Trained staff were scarce, and there was some concern to try and avoid over-use of the new orders by enthusiastic youth courts. In many areas, therefore, reparation orders were phased in gradually and on a small scale.

While this delay may not have reflected government policy, it will probably prove to have been wise. Reparation orders require substantial staff time if they are to be implemented effectively, and youth offending teams need to ensure that they are not made in too great numbers. There is also a case for ensuring that the orders are not given to unduly minor offenders, for whom there is a range of other, less intrusive, forms of intervention.

Some youth offending teams have implemented reparation orders only in respect of young offenders who have identifiable, personal victims. Elsewhere, however, imaginative schemes have been developed which allow young people's awareness of the implications of property crime with corporate victims to be raised. Because of the volume of work, some Teams have introduced small group work which allows young people to be seen quickly after their court appearances, and to be encouraged to think about the effects of their offending upon themselves and others.

The **final warnings** which have largely replaced the previous system of police cautioning have been used in large numbers by courts in many areas. They still include a formal warning from a senior police officer, but they also involve a follow-up interview with a member of the youth offending team (who in many areas is also a police officer). This means that detailed assessments have to be completed on all such young people, and the instrument that staff are required to use is cumbersome and intrusive for this purpose. There is a danger that the completion of a lengthy risk assessment form may get in the way of more constructive intervention, and that some of the questions (for example about drug use, offending by family members, and sexual behaviour) are intrusive and inappropriate for young people who have mostly committed very minor offences. There must also be a concern that the 12-page ASSET assessment form collects a good deal of information which official agencies have no right to know when assessing minor delinquency.

What we know about what works

The question of 'what works' in youth justice is a controversial one. While there is a body of knowledge about effective practice with adult offenders (McGuire, 1995; Underdown, 1998), it is to some extent contested (Mair, 1997; Fraser, 2000) and the attempt to implement 'what works' has been largely politically driven. There has been less research on effective practice with younger offenders, and much of it is American and 'may not be especially relevant to the kinds of offender sentenced to community penalties in the United Kingdom' (Mair, 1997).

In general terms, we know something about what does not work with young offenders:

- Intensive intervention should not be targeted at minor offenders as it may make matters worse (Haines and Drakeford, 1998).
- Shaming young offenders is unlikely to be helpful unless it occurs within a reintegrative framework. Shame is more likely to be effectively mobilised in respect of personal rather than institutional victims, and lecturing young offenders in a humiliating way is unlikely to improve their attitudes (Braithwaite, 1999).
- Institutionalising young people is less effective than working with them in the community (Audit Commission, 1996).

As for effective practice in working with victims of crime, it is clearly established that:

- Family group conferences involving victims can make possible a healing process for both offenders and victims (McElrea, 1996), although careful procedures are required to protect the rights and interests of each (Morris and Maxwell, 2000).
- In the case of minor offending, other models of mediation may be helpful both to victims and to offenders, but the effectiveness of restorative justice in the UK is limited by grafting it onto a retributive criminal justice system (Zedner, 1997), and in the circumstances it might have been best to reserve restorative approaches for relatively serious offenders. Widespread experimentation with victim-offender mediation is taking place in Europe, but the results of evaluative research will not be available for some time.
- Young people suffer disproportionately as victims of crime, but UK youth justice policy has so far concentrated upon the 'youth crime problem' at the expense of the 'youth victimisation problem' (Furlong and Cartmel, 1997).
- Rather than being completely separate and mutually exclusive groups, many offenders have experienced victimisation and many victims have themselves previously committed offences (Peelo et al., 1992; Boswell, 1999).
- The fact that there are overlaps between the categories of victim and offender suggests a cautious approach to visiting victims in their own homes without first checking whether they are known to the police or probation services (HMIP, 2000).

- Current provision for supporting the victims of racist crime and for official recognition of the diversity of crime victims is inadequate (HMIP, 2000; Macpherson, 1999). Services to victims need to be designed in such a way as to remedy these deficiencies.
- Raising victims' expectations without meeting them inevitably makes matters worse (Hoyle et al., 1998), and this should be borne in mind in designing projects. Consultation with a range of victims' organisations can be extremely helpful in this respect. Victims of crime expect, but do not always receive, information about the progress of the case against 'their' offender. They may express their anger at the way they have been treated to any representative of the criminal justice system who contacts them, and youth justice staff need to be prepared for this, and for the information-providing role (Williams, 1999b).

Good practice

These research findings provide some limited pointers towards good practice in implementing the 1998 Crime and Disorder Act and the 1999 Youth Justice and Criminal Evidence Act in England and Wales. For a summary of the various new disposals involving victims, and some of the issues they raise for practice, see Williams, 2000. At the risk of stating the obvious, this section draws out some of the implications of the research for practice under the new arrangements.

Staff training seems likely to be a key issue, as it was in the probation service when its responsibilities for work with victims of crime suddenly increased in the early 1990s (Williams, 1999; HMIP, 2000). Both professional and administrative staff require preparation and training for work with victims. They need to be aware of the feelings aroused by victimisation, and brief *victim awareness* courses are useful for this purpose. Local Victim Support schemes are experienced in providing these, as are more specialist agencies such as Women's Aid, Rape Crisis and racial harassment groups. There is a case for providing such training to all who may come into contact with victims or refer young offenders for reparative interventions. Once there is a basic level of victim awareness within agencies, more specialised training can usefully be provided. Staff directly involved in work with offenders and victims need an understanding of *the underlying principles of restorative justice*, as set out, for example, by the Restorative Justice Consortium (undated), and Marshall and Merry (1990). The latter provides a succinct summary of the main principles of victim/offender mediation:

- **Offenders** should be held accountable for the harm they cause and do as much as they can to put things right with the victim.
- **Victims** should be empowered to take an active role in the criminal process.
- **Citizens** should play an active role in crime prevention and local social control (1990).

Staff can then begin to get to grips with the *range of models of restorative justice* currently operating here and overseas.

Without this understanding, there is a danger that different projects around the country re-invent the wheel in slightly differing ways, and that practice fails to follow the basic principles and standards developed as a result of experience elsewhere. This is not to say that the RJC standards are written on tablets of stone. Rather, projects need to be able to justify any decisions which depart from the established principles. Such decisions should not be taken in ignorance of the range of possibilities.

Once staff have a reasonable level of victim awareness, they need training for the specific tasks involved in working with victims or victim issues. They may need reassurance that their existing skills in working with young offenders are transferable to work with victims: previous experience and research suggests that they are (see Williams, 1999a). Such training should also encourage staff to reflect upon the implications of research, which shows that victims and offenders are overlapping, rather than discrete, groups. For instance, what does one do when a victim awareness session turns into a disclosure of abuse? Some issues for the management and practice of work with victims are closely linked to questions of training, and there is likely to be a need for further training as this area of work develops. A number of national bodies now offer staff training programmes.

Proper **preparation** before victims and offenders are invited to become involved in reparative work is essential. Staff training needs to emphasise the importance of such preparatory work. Victims must always be fully consulted before reparative interventions are set up, and in many cases this will take time, and require more than one meeting. The procedural rights of both victims and offenders must be respected if constructive outcomes are to be achieved. In the context of the Human Rights Act 1998, this becomes even more important. The Act, in force from 2 October 2000, incorporates the European Convention on Human Rights into the law of England and Wales. This means that breaches of rights such as that to respect for privacy, access to legal assistance, and due process can be challenged in our own courts (Justice, 2000).

It may be necessary to **negotiate with the courts** in order to ensure that the need for such preparatory work is understood and respected. Local victims' organisations may be of assistance in this process. In some areas, youth offending teams have arranged joint training sessions for their own staff and youth court magistrates, and this would appear to be a useful model. Quite apart from the training needs of YOT staff, there is a huge training agenda associated with this legislation for sentencers. Many staff and magistrates have little understanding of the principles underlying restorative justice (Dignan, 2000). It can be a two-way process: in many areas, the magistrates have received extensive preparatory training about the human rights legislation and its implications for criminal courts.

YOT managers will find it helpful to **involve a range of local victim support agencies** in the development of work with victims. While Victim Support is often the most professionalised and accessible, it cannot be assumed to speak for all victims of crime, and there is a strong case for opening channels of communication with other groups such as Women's Aid, Rape Crisis, inter-agency domestic violence forums, racial harassment groups and other self-help organisations (Williams, 1999b).

Despite the repeated political messages that non-intervention is no longer appropriate, there is a continuing need to **target intervention in order to avoid net-widening**. In the new legislative framework, this will not always be easy, but the effectiveness literature does stress the need to keep intervention to a level commensurate with the seriousness of the risk presented by each offender, as does the Criminal Justice Act 1991. Some of the new Orders are so resource-intensive that it will, in any case, be essential to limit their use. Otherwise, teams will be overwhelmed by the volume of work. Here again, early negotiations with the courts will pay off.

Appropriate priority will need to be given to work with **victims of racial harassment and abuse**. This requires good relationships with other agencies and the appointment of an appropriate range of staff, as well as ready access to interpreters where required.

On the level of individual practice, a number of pointers to good practice emerge from the literature and the experience of the pilot YOTs. Where reparative interventions are designed to elicit shame on the part of young offenders, it is vital that this is done in a context of **reintegrative shaming**. This suggests that reparation orders, for example, should not normally be used where there is no personal victim: the evidence is that institutional victims may not always be sympathetic to the principles of restorative justice. Young people will not change their attitudes if they are humiliated as part of a reparation project (Marshall and Merry, 1990; Young and Goold, 1999). However, there are more constructive and informal ways of approaching reparation to institutional victims, as the Milton Keynes Retail Theft Initiative (MKRTI) has shown (Justice, 2000). Note, however, the concerns raised in the Justice report about the lack of procedural safeguards in the MKRTI as originally implemented (Justice, 2000). Routine, bureaucratic approaches will be perceived as inauthentic by young offenders, and the use of strategies such as encouraging young people to write letters of apology needs to be kept under review.

Keeping victims informed may sometimes be the responsibility of other agencies. The research evidence is that they have not made a very good job of it (Macpherson, 1999; Williams, 1999, 1999b; HMIP, 2000). Where it is the responsibility of a youth offending team, it should be given a very high priority, and administrative systems should be designed to ensure that victims are told what progress is being made once they have been offered services. Lack of information contributes significantly to a sense of being re-victimised by the system. Individual staff working with victims should go out of their way to avoid this (and victim awareness training should emphasise the information issues).

As noted above, practitioners should **recognise the overlapping nature of the categories of** 'victim' and 'offender'. We know from the research that many victims have previously offended, and many offenders are former victims. This should influence staff attitudes to health and safety (leading them to be as circumspect about visiting previously unknown victims at home as they are in the case of offenders; see HMIP, 2000). It should also influence the design of services: for example, it may be necessary to provide one-to-one support for young people involved in group work, in case they have previously been victimised themselves.

Finally, practitioners need to **be critical of what they are told about research evidence and** 'what works'. Reading much of the Home Office 'what works' literature, one could be forgiven for thinking that the successes of youth justice in the 1980s and early 1990s had never happened (Haines and Drakeford, 1998). As recently as 1996, the Audit Commission was quoting research which showed that cautioning was effective (Audit Commission, 1996). The reason for the sudden change of direction over the succeeding two years was political, not research-driven. Similarly, it is simplistic to argue that young people no longer grow out of crime: the research evidence is that it now takes longer than it once did. That does not necessarily imply, as some have argued, that it is indefensible not to intervene intensively in young people's lives at an early stage. It certainly does not mean that incarcerating more young people will improve matters. Indeed, a central message of the 'what works' literature is that incarceration should be a last resort, because it is so destructive. Practitioners will do well to remember what has been learnt over the last decades.

Conclusion

The design and delivery of appropriate services to victims of crime creates a huge workload, at the very time when local youth offending teams have least time to give to it. Other priorities are just as pressing. YOT managers can only keep so many different plates spinning at a time.

However, it is crucial that this part of the jigsaw of new disposals and new ways of working is in place at an early stage, and that it fits smoothly with other parts of the system. The importance of making a good job of work with victims is obvious, and the victim movement has shown enormous interest in and good will towards the new reparative approach.

Staff in all parts of the youth justice system need proper preparation and training for their new responsibilities in respect of victims of crime. This should include an understanding of the messages of research (which are complex, subtle and sometimes contradictory) and an appreciation of the wide range of possible ways of delivering reparative work. We should build on what we know about 'what works', but with due modesty. The process of building up that knowledge base is at a very early stage.

References

Audit Commission (1996) *Misspent Youth: Young People and Crime.* Audit Commission.

Boswell, G. (1999) Young Offenders who Commit Grave Crimes: The Criminal Justice Response, in Kemshall, H. and Pritchard, J. (Eds.) *Good Practice in Working with Violence.* Jessica Kingsley.

Braithwaite, J. (1989) *Crime, Shame and Reintegration.* Cambridge University Press.

Braithwaite, J. (1999) Restorative Justice: Assessing Optimistic and Pessimistic Accounts, in Tonry, M. (Ed.) *Crime and Justice: A Review of Research.* University of Chicago Press.

Crawford, A. and Enterkin, J. (forthcoming) Victim Contact Work in the Probation Service: Paradigm Shift or Pandora's Box? *British Journal of Criminology.*

Dignan, J. (1999) *Draft Interim Report on the Reparative Work being Undertaken by Youth Offending Teams.* University of Sheffield.

Dignan, J. (2000) *Youth Justice Pilots Evaluation: Interim Report on Reparative Work and Youth Offending Teams.* Home Office.

Fattah, E. A. (1998) Some Reflections on the Paradigm of Restorative Justice and its Viability for Juvenile Justice, in Walgrave, L. (Ed.) *Restorative Justice for Juveniles: Potentialities, Risks and Problems.* Leuven University Press.

Fraser, D. (2000) A Critique of Research Related to 'What Works' in Reducing Offending. *Justice of the Peace.* 164, May, 356–9.

Furlong, A. and Cartmel, F. (1997) *Young People and Social Change: Individualisation and Risk in Late Modernity.* Open University Press.

Gatti, U. and Ceretti, A. (1998) Italian experiences of victim-offender mediation in the juvenile justice system, in Walgrave, L. (Ed.) *Restorative Justice for Juveniles: Potentialities, Risks and Problems.* Leuven University Press.

Haines, K. and Drakeford, M. (1998) *Young People and Youth Justice*. Macmillan.

HM Inspectorate of Probation (2000) *The Victim Perspective: Ensuring the Victim Matters*. Thematic Inspection Report. Home Office.

Hoyle, C., Cape, E., Morgan, R.. and Sanders, A. (1998*) Evaluation of the 'One Stop Shop' and Victim Statement pilot projects*. Home Office.

Jackson, S. E. (1999) Family Group Conferences and Youth Justice: The New Panacea? in Goldson, B. (Ed.) *Youth Justice: Contemporary Policy and Practice*. Ashgate.

Justice (2000) *Restoring Youth Justice: New Directions in Domestic and International Law and Practice*. Justice.

Lindstrom, P. and Svanberg, K. (1998) Victim-offender Mediation In Sweden, A Research Note, in Walgrave, L. (Ed.) *Restorative Justice for Juveniles: Potentialities, Risks and Problems*. Leuven University Press.

McElrea, F. (1996) The New Zealand Youth Court: A Model for Use with Adults, in Galaway, B. and Hudson, J. (Eds.) *Restorative Justice: International Perspectives*. Kugler.

McEvoy, K. and Gormally, B. (2000) *State, Community and the 'Ownership' of Restorative Justice: Initial Reflections upon the Criminal Justice Review in Northern Ireland*. Unpublished paper given at the annual conference of the Socio-legal Studies Association, Belfast, 27 April.

McGuire, J. (1995) (Ed.) *What Works: Reducing Reoffending*. John Wiley.

Macpherson, W. (1999) *The Stephen Lawrence Inquiry Report*. Cm. 4262. Stationery Office.

Mair, G. (1997) Community Penalties and the Probation Service, in Maguire, M., Morgan, R. and Reiner, R., *The Oxford Handbook of Criminology*. 2nd edn. Clarendon.

Marshall, T. F. and Merry, S. (1990) *Crime and Accountability: Victim/Offender Mediation in Practice*. HMSO.

Morris, A. and Maxwell, G. (2000) The Practice of Family Group Conferences in New Zealand: Assessing the Place, Potential and Pitfalls of Restorative Justice, in Crawford, A. and Goodey, J. (Eds.) *Integrating a Victim Perspective within Criminal Justice*. Ashgate.

Muncie, J. (1999) *Youth and Crime: a Critical Introduction*. Sage.

Peelo, M., Stewart, J., Stewart, G. and Prior, A. (1992) *A Sense of Justice: Offenders as Victims of Crime*. Association of Chief Officers of Probation.

Restorative Justice Consortium (undated) *Standards for Restorative Justice*. RJC.

Schelkens, W. (1998) Community Service and Mediation in the Juvenile Justice Legislation in Europe, in Walgrave, L. (Ed.) *Restorative Justice for Juveniles: Potentialities, Risks and Problems*. Leuven University Press.

Umbreit, M., Bradshaw, W. and Coates, R. B. (1999) Victims of Severe Violence Meet the Offender: Restorative Justice Through Dialogue. *International Review of Victimology*. 6 (4) 321–43.

Underdown, A. (1998) *Strategies for Effective Offender Supervision*. HM Inspectorate of Probation.

Williams, B. (1999) The Victim's Charter: Citizens as Consumers of Criminal Justice. *Howard Journal of Criminal Justice*. 38 (4) 384–96.

Williams, B. (1999a) Youth Offending Teams and Work with Victims of Crime. *Ajjust Now*. 44, August.

Williams, B. (1999b) *Working with Victims of Crime: Policies, Politics and Practice*. Jessica Kingsley.

Williams, B. (2000) Victims of Crime and the New Youth Justice, in Goldson, B. (Ed.) *The New Youth Justice*. Russell House Publishing.

Young, R. (2000) Integrating a Multi-victim Perspective into Criminal Justice Through Restorative Justice Conferences, in Crawford, A. and Goodey, J. (Eds.) *Integrating a Victim Perspective within Criminal Justice*. Ashgate.

Young, R. and Goold, B. (1999) Restorative Police Cautioning in Aylesbury: From Degrading to Reintegrative Shaming Ceremonies? *Criminal Law Review*. 126–38.

Youth Justice Board (2000) *National Standards for Youth Justice*. Youth Justice Board/Home Office/Department for Education and Employment/Department of Health/Lord Chancellor's Department/National Assembly for Wales.

Zedner, L. (1997) Victims, in Maguire, M., Morgan, R. and Reiner, R., *The Oxford Handbook of Criminology*. 2nd edn. Clarendon.

CHAPTER 10

The school, youth crime and violent victimisation

John Pitts

Introduction

This chapter gives an account of an action research project that aimed to reduce the violent victimisation of school students. It was undertaken in schools in London and Merseyside in the mid 1990s. On average, people spend over 15,000 hours of their lives in school (Rutter et al., 1986). Next to the family, the school is the institution likely to have the greatest impact on a child or young person's development. As a result social scientists have been keen to understand the relationship between schooling, youth crime and youth victimisation.

The delinquescent school

Research undertaken by Power, Benn and Norris (1972) in East London in the 1960s and 1970s revealed that the likelihood of a young person appearing in a juvenile court was profoundly dependent upon which school they attended. This led Power and his colleagues to posit the existence of what they described as the *delinquescent* school, one which either fostered, or failed to prevent, tendencies towards criminality in school students. Farrington and West (1993) in their Cambridge Study of Delinquent Development found that attending a 'high delinquency school' correlated with later convictions. However, they argued that because the most troublesome children went on to attend the highest delinquency schools, it was the children not the schools which determined the differential delinquency rates. However, as John Graham has observed:

> Longitudinal studies have tended to neglect the influence of schools in the development of delinquent careers. Rutter et al. (1979) pointed out that, on closer examination of the Cambridge data, some school variation independent of intake is perceptible, with a slightly higher tendency for boys with 'average' behaviour at primary school to become delinquent at high delinquency schools than low delinquency schools. (Graham, 1998)

So what is it about schools which promote or discourage involvement in crime?

Michael Rutter and his colleagues (1987) suggested that the structure and ethos of schools can have a significant impact upon attendance, attainment, behaviour in class, levels of violent victimisation and student involvement in crime. In a similar vein, Olweus (1989) suggests that structure, culture and patterns of communication have a significant impact on the conduct of students. Recent UK initiatives have aimed to increase participation by students, enhance their study skills, increase teachers' inter-personal competence and cultivate pride in the school and these have led to decreases in 'self-report delinquency' (Graham, 1988; Pitts and Smith 1995).

Whole school 'anti-violent victimisation' initiatives of the type outlined in Figure 1 (below) have also been shown to reduce violence in schools and in the catchment areas around schools (Graham, 1988; Olweus, 1989; Pitts and Smith, 1995). We also know that in high crime neighbourhoods, behaviour in and out of school is closely linked and that effective intervention in the school to improve communication between staff and students, clarify expectations, rewards and sanctions and offer training and support to staff and students can have a marked effect upon youth violence (Graham, 1988).

A whole-school initiative to reduce the violent victimisation of children and young people in a high crime neighbourhood

In the 1990s the present author was involved in a violence reduction initiative, based in two primary schools and two secondary schools in high crime neighbourhoods, in East London and

---

Figure 1: Whole-school Anti-bullying Programmes (Olweus, 1989)

General prerequisites
1. awareness of the problem
2. involvement in devising solutions

Measures at school level
1. questionnaire survey
2. structured school-wide discussion of bully/victim problems
3. improved supervision and surveillance of play areas during breaks
4. more attractive play areas or broader range of break activities
5. confidential contact for victims and others concerning bullying
6. meetings about bullying between staff and parents
7. teacher working parties on strategies for developing positive social relationships between students

Measures at class level
1. class rules against bullying: clarification of proscribed behaviour, praise for non-bullying behaviour and the development of realistic and mutually agreed sanctions
2. regular class meetings
3. role-playing and using literature which highlights the plight of scapegoated groups and individuals
4. encouraging co-operative, as opposed to competitive learning
5. shared positive class activities, trips, parties etc.

Measures at individual level
1. formal confrontations of students who bully
2. formal meetings with students' parents
3. encouragement of 'neutral' students to help
4. encouragement of parents to help, through production of informal folders, contact telephone numbers etc.
5. organising discussion groups for parents of students who bully or are bullied
6. devising clear and quick procedures for a change of class or school, should this prove necessary

Merseyside, with particular problems of violence (Pitts 1993; Pitts and Smith 1995). The initiative utilised participative action-research to devise anti-victimisation strategies with school students.

The research team adopted an Organisational Development (OD) approach to the task. OD proceeds from the assumption that the policy objectives of complex 'human service' organisations are most likely to be realised if they win the support, and articulate the interests, of members of that organisation at all levels. This support is gained by a process of continuous consultation and it is this 'process' which holds the key to the success of OD. As Diana Robbins (1989) suggests, the most important aspect of policies will often be the impact that the process of their formulation has on the culture and ethos of the organisation.

The researchers believed that OD offered a way of identifying and working with those features of the school which promoted, or inhibited, violent victimisation. Their beliefs about what these features were, derived from their experiences as workers in the justice, care and educational systems, and research evidence about the development and operation of violent subcultures in prisons and residential establishments (Mathiesen, 1964; Jones, 1968; Millham et al., 1975; Dennington and Pitts, 1991).

In brief, this work suggests that violent victimisation is most likely to occur in institutions where:
- There is an extensive and rigid hierarchy in which information flow from those at the bottom to those at the top of the hierarchy is poor.
- Individual members of staff, who are the organisation's culture carriers, pursue incompatible goals and espouse or enact conflicting values.
- The deployment of rewards and punishments appears to be arbitrary and done without reference to a common standard or set of rules.
- Staff appear to be indifferent to violent behaviour not directed at themselves.
- There are few expressions of warmth between people at different levels of the organisation.

Conversely, violent victimisation will be least likely to occur in an organisation where:
- There is a relatively flat hierarchy in which information flow upwards and downwards is maximised and where that information affects decisions made by staff.
- Staff, in consultation with other members of the organisation, have regular opportunities to discuss goals and values and participate in policy formulation.
- The deployment of rewards and punishments is seen to be fair and proportional and corresponds with standards or rules to which members of the organisation at all levels can subscribe.
- Staff are actively concerned about violent behaviour.
- There are frequent, spontaneous, expressions of warmth between people at different levels of the hierarchy.

The goal of OD is to facilitate the movement of the organisation along the continuum from the former type of organisational structure, towards the latter. While violent victimisation, and other anti-social behaviour in schools, do not simply originate within the school, research suggests that the structure of a school, and the culture it generates, can either contain and reduce, or exacerbate, such behaviour (Hargreaves, 1967; Power et al., 1972; Rutter et al., 1978).

The initiative had five broad objectives:

1. To produce an anti-violent victimisation code of practice and a strategy for its implementation through a process of staff/student consultation and collaboration.
2. To increase the awareness and knowledge of teachers and students about violence in and out of school.
3. To maximise the involvement of teachers, supervisory staff and relevant community groups and agencies in the prevention of violent victimisation amongst young people.
4. To improve the monitoring and supervision of students by adults, especially in the playground and on the way to and from school in order to deter, and intervene to prevent, violent victimisation.
5. To maximise support for victims from staff and non-violent and non-victimised students.

Victimisation

Although the primary concern of the project was the violent victimisation of children and young people, we were aware that students were concerned about a range of issues concerning their safety and security and we therefore encouraged students to talk about them in a self-report questionnaire.

Across all the schools, *in London and Merseyside*, the most common form of victimisation experienced by students was name-calling. In London, having your family 'cussed' and racist taunts featured prominently. About half of the primary school students and about a quarter of secondary students had been 'hit or kicked' by a fellow student in the preceding year. Boys were consistently more likely than girls to have experienced physical violence, while girls were disproportionately likely to have experienced being given dirty looks or having stories told about them. In the London schools however, it is clear that non-white students were disproportionately violently victimised. In responding to the question of how frequently they had been bullied, students were free to apply their own definition of what constituted bullying while elsewhere in the questionnaire they were presented with a range of violent victimisation behaviours: physical violence; threats; name calling; being ignored; having belongings taken. They were invited to tick a box if they had experienced any of these. Students identified physical violence, threats and verbal abuse as being the core elements of violence. This survey showed that there was a significant amount of violent victimisation in all schools with a greater concentration at primary level. There was noticeably more weekly violent victimisation in the London primary school, although violent victimisation was remarkably consistent at around 16 per cent in both primary schools and 5-6 per cent in both secondary schools. Violent victimisation was most prevalent in the primary schools and appears to reduce as students' progress through the secondary schools. However, the violence tended to be more serious amongst the older age group and the researchers felt that many older boys were reluctant to admit that they had been picked upon.

The process

The key elements in the process were to facilitate communication between all members of the school community and to harness their collective resources in combating violent victimisation. Whilst good communication and co-operation are central features of any organisational task, they are particularly pertinent to an anti-violence initiative. Violent victimisation thrives in an atmosphere of secrecy; victims and bystanders fear reprisals if they report an incident. Without knowledge of the incident, staff cannot intervene to protect the victim and, accordingly, young people do not see them as an effective source of help to which they can turn. All members of the school community can easily become trapped in this cycle and become resigned to their own powerlessness. It was a priority for the initiative team, to create structures which would enable such fatalism to be overcome. In each school, consultative exercises were designed, to enable members at all levels to analyse the problem and to devise collective responses to it. In this way the strategies which emerged were relevant to the particular circumstances of the school concerned and, importantly, all members of the school community could experience ownership of the endeavour.

In advance of the project the schools involved were sent details of the initiative. The subsequent stages of the consultation process, outlined below, were broadly similar in the Merseyside primary and secondary schools and the London secondary school. For reasons which will be explained later, intervention in the London primary school followed a different pattern. In the annexe to this chapter, actual details of the consultation exercise are reproduced.

1. Discussion with the head/deputy
Our initial discussions with senior staff in the schools aimed to transmit information about the methods and the techniques that the initiative team could employ and the nature and duration of the involvement of staff and students. The meeting was used to establish a timetable and nominate a senior member of staff who would be the link with the initiative team. It emerged subsequently that the authority ceded by heads to the person occupying this role, their own commitment to the project, and the extent to which they were trusted by staff and students, held the key to effective intervention.

2. Meetings with staff
In their subsequent meetings with the whole staff group, the project team used a variety of whole-group exercises to establish participants' beliefs, fears and fantasies about their schools, and their knowledge and understanding of the 'official' procedures and practices relating to violent victimisation. At these meetings staff were asked to nominate representatives for a staff working party.

3. Introduction to year groups
The initiative was introduced to the whole school in a series of year assemblies. At these assemblies, the behaviours which constituted violent victimisation, and their consequences for victims were outlined by a member of the initiative team. Students were then asked to nominate two volunteers from each class to join a year group working party.

4. Staff and year group working parties
Two volunteers from each class in each year met for three sessions with a member of the research team who acted as a facilitator and recorded the participants' deliberations. Using case study material and age-appropriate exercises, these groups discussed the problems of, and their preferred solutions to, violent victimisation and violence in the school and the local community. In parallel with this, there were three 'problem-solving sessions' with the staff working party.

5. Staff-student anti-violence working party
In the secondary schools, staff-student anti-violence working parties were established. This comprised student representatives from each year, members of staff from each year, the deputy

head and a researcher who acted as secretary. The task of the working parties was to operationalise and monitor the anti-violence policy and the strategies adopted by staff and students.

Work in the schools

The London primary school
This was the smallest of the four schools involved in the project and had a 'familial' atmosphere. Teaching staff worked closely with a team of 'helpers' who carried out playground duty and offered additional adult support during lessons. In the early stages of the project, initiative workers spent sessions with the whole staff group. There was considerable debate about the tension staff experienced between administering a set of rules, which were fair and consistent, and being able to remain responsive to the needs of particular children. Initiative workers and staff spent time attempting to develop systems which accommodated both imperatives.

It became clear, however, that staff, together with some students and parents, had only recently been involved in a consultative exercise aimed at drawing up a behavioural policy for the school. They therefore had little enthusiasm for engaging in further consultation that appeared to duplicate work already undertaken. However, there was interest in exploiting the medium of video in work with children to reinforce their understanding of, and commitment to, the new behavioural policy. This work was undertaken in two stages.

In the first stage, members of the initiative team held a series of 'workshops', each with a different group of four to six children. Each group was told that it could use video to put together a 'programme' about violent victimisation. Invariably groups chose to construct role-play featuring a violent incident. They engaged in this with considerable enthusiasm and required only minimal directorial guidance. Playback of the role-plays allowed opportunity for analysis of how and why the dramatised events had developed in the ways they did, and was used to prompt discussion and exploration of such questions as:

- What could or should the aggressor and victim have done in that situation?
- How could that type of situation be prevented?
- Who has responsibility for preventing violent victimisation?
- How can victims be better protected?
- How should people who are violent to other children be dealt with?

The readiness with which the children engaged in these workshops, and their obvious enjoyment in doing so, endorsed our view that video was a useful medium for opening up discussion about violent victimisation and related issues. The camera acted as a catalyst in this process.

As a follow-up to this series of workshops, and drawing upon ideas that emerged from them, staff and students worked with the researchers to produce a video which was to be shown to new entrants to the school to introduce them to the behaviour policy and the violent victimisation elements within it. This involved more considered preparation than the earlier impromptu role-plays. Staff and students collaborated in the production of a script and rehearsals before scenes were shot. The material they produced was subsequently edited and has been shown to children joining the school.

The production of the video served as a vehicle whereby new channels of communication between staff and students could be established. It was therefore crucially important that, in the production of the video tape, the children engaged in active and frequent consultation with other students, ancillary and teaching staff and the school head, in order to agree a script and the ways in which staff responses should be portrayed. The making of the video created a forum for a debate about what action needed to be taken, who should take it and whose interests these actions should serve. This mode of intervention was well suited to the primary school in which sustained debate and protracted discussion in working parties, as happened in the secondary schools, would not have been appropriate. The video allowed us to *formulate crucial questions in an explicit way* and engage key people in the organisation in their clarification and resolution. Moreover, it enabled us to do this while according a central role to school students and staying within their experience.

Children's responses to the three questionnaires covering the two year period of the project, indicated a decrease in the percentage of children who were victimised regularly ('every week' or 'most days') and an increase in the percentage of children who had not been victimised.

The trend towards a decrease in bullying was also apparent from the children's responses to the question asking how frequently they had bullied other students during the preceding three months. The number of students who admitted having done so fell from around 40 to 25 per cent.

A major factor associated with the decrease in victimisation in this school appeared to be children's perceptions of the extent to which staff would intervene to prevent it. Both teachers and ancillary workers (or 'dinner ladies') were seen as much more proactive in the second self-report questionnaires completed by students. Interestingly, as victimisation decreased children's self-esteem appeared to rise. In the second questionnaire a higher proportion of children saw themselves as being able to do things 'very well'. Moreover, a significantly lower percentage 'bunked off school'. These findings offer some support for the notion that victimisation is less likely to occur when children feel confident in their abilities and contented in the school environment.

The Merseyside primary school
Although this school was somewhat larger than the London primary school, researchers found that it shared some of the 'familial' characteristics. Teachers knew the children well, and many parents had themselves previously been students at the school. The school was an established landmark in the local community.

Notwithstanding, at the onset of the project, this school had the highest percentage of children who were victimised. Very quickly the researchers picked up on the children's sense of distress at the levels of victimisation in the school. A researcher was addressing a whole school assembly to explain the project and talk about victimisation, when she was interrupted by a child putting up her hand and saying: 'It's happening here . . . Now . . . At this moment.' After the assembly, a group of children approached the initiative worker to elaborate upon their concerns. From this, and subsequent small group meetings with students, it was clear that they had a lot to say about victimisation but lacked the confidence to bring their concerns into a public arena.

Taking a cue from this and in consultation with staff at the school, the researchers set up a programme of peer education. This involved older students working with younger ones on questions of what constituted victimisation, students' feelings about it, their responses to it and the rules and procedures the school had developed to deal with it. Peer education has its origins in the work of Paolo Friere and Ivan Illich and their attempts to devise a 'pedagogy of the oppressed'. It attaches importance to the experiential learning of people in similar situations and the ways in which the experiences of those who have passed through oppressive situations can be reformulated to serve as a support and guide for those who find themselves in similar situations. This process offers benefits to both parties. It offers the mentor an affirmation that they have successfully negotiated and survived damaging experiences thus consolidating a positive self image, while for the other participant, the mentor serves as a support and an example that difficulties, that may at that moment seem overwhelming, can be overcome. This mode of learning, which aims to increase communication between, and confidence among students, initially met with some resistance from staff. They said that it was their job to teach and that this role could not, and should not, be handed over to relatively young children. When, after protracted discussion with the research team, the idea was re-presented by the deputy head as a means of developing peer leadership, it was accepted more readily.

The researchers held the view that it was contradictory to expect children and young people to assume responsibility for their own behaviour, and that of others, if they were not given the means and the authority to do so. Yet, it is a process which necessarily requires adults to relinquish some of their own control and authority and this can be an anxiety-provoking business. As children gained in confidence, there was greater disclosure of victimisation.

There was little improvement in students' reports of bullying at the end of the first year of the project. It was only in the subsequent year that we saw a significant decrease in victimisation, with those reporting that they had not been violently victimised rising from 28.4 to 51.7 per cent. A factor which appears to be closely associated with the reduction in victimisation is the increased willingness of students to report to staff that they have been bullied. Our data gives some support to the view that the decrease in victimisation was associated with this pupil-led initiative in reporting incidents more frequently. In contrast with the other primary school, there was no marked difference over the period in the frequency with which students perceived teachers intervening to stop victimisation.

The Merseyside secondary school
It took some time for the research team and school staff to find common ground in this school. Staff had been led to believe that the researchers would prescribe victimisation-reduction strategies which the school would simply implement. The research team, on the other hand, were concerned that 'solutions' should emerge from a whole-school consultative process which involved the students.

Eventually, the impasse was resolved when staff and a researcher undertook joint work on developing an eight-session Assertiveness and Empowerment module for the Personal and Social Education curriculum. This module was pursued by all students and dealt with self-esteem, assertiveness, prejudice, stereotyping, conflict and its creative resolution. Throughout, the course focused on individual, group and class-wide strategies which could be utilised to deal with conflict, allow authentic communication and counter racism, sexism and other forms of prejudice. The positive aspect of this approach to the problem of bullying is that it establishes the issue firmly in the curriculum in a way that all staff and students can use, and provides a vehicle by which channels of communication between staff and students can be opened up.

Over the period, violent victimisation diminished significantly in the Merseyside secondary school. It appeared that shifts in boys', rather than girls', attitudes and behaviour were the key factor in this reduction. In the first questionnaire 74 per cent of boys had expressed the view that violent victimisation was 'wrong'. In the final questionnaire 84 per cent did. The percentage of girls who held this view remained high but relatively static: 93 and 90 per cent. Over the period, the percentage of boys who admitted victimising others dropped from 33 to 25 per cent. For girls the percentage figures were 15 and 12 per cent respectively.

Since most victimisation by boys is against other boys, the reduction meant that boys were victimised less. Over the two-year period the percentage of boys who were victimised 'mainly by one boy' fell from 10 to 6 per cent. Experience of victimisation by 'many boys' fell from 15 to 9 per cent and victimisation by a 'gang' from 11 to 5 per cent.

The London secondary school
At the inception of the project, racial tension and general turbulence at the school were high. Over the preceding two years there had been a significant increase in the numbers, and the proportion, of Bangladeshi students from beyond the local estate entering Year 7. Whereas in some local schools Bangladeshi students constituted over 80 per cent of the school roll, for some years the figure in this school had remained at around 40 per cent. In consequence, it had become a 'white flight' school, popular with some influential white residents who saw it as 'their' school, to which, they believed, 'their' children should have a right of access. At the same time, there had been an increase in the proportion of students with 'behavioural problems' entering the school and an already over-stretched staff group was beginning to feel the strain.

These pressures had led to a feeling amongst staff that the school was no longer a 'safe place'. The most tangible expression of this perceived threat came from a group of adolescents who tended to loiter around the school entrance. Some of them were unemployed ex-students and others were students who had been permanently excluded for violent or threatening behaviour towards staff or other students. They were often drunk or 'stoned' and were intimidating to staff and students. It was the belief of some local police officers, local agencies and members of staff that some of these youths were involved, and may well have been the prime movers, in racial attacks and other violent incidents on the estate.

Whatever the reality, their presence as bearers of the culture of violence and as a symbol of divisions and antagonisms in the community, cast an aura upon the school. David Downes (1990) refers to an incident at the school in 1990 in which a fight between a white and a Bangladeshi student erupted into an orchestrated 'theatre of violence'. The incident culminated in a pitched battle in the local market, but few of the axe and mallet-brandishing protagonists were from the school. Students were aware that, increasingly, violence against the Bangladeshi community was being met by reprisals from groups of young Bangladeshi men known as the 'Rock Street Mafia'. Whether the Rock Street Mafia' actually existed, or was simply shorthand for a rising generation of Bangladeshi young people who fought back, is not clear. Whatever the reality however, each side demanded racial loyalty. Pupils of all races felt intimidated and under pressure to take sides, even though most of them wanted no part in the conflict.

Inevitably, these pressures from outside the school found expression in behaviour inside the school. Year 7 students, talking to their group facilitators, said:

People bully mainly because of racist reasons, white boys beat up Bangladeshi boys for no reason other than their skin colour.

Nonetheless, students also talked about the ways in which racism and violence, both within the school and beyond it, could be countered:

> . . . this led on to a discussion of what the school could do to help young people argue against becoming involved in racial conflict. They felt that they needed ammunition to use against bigots: some of them said that this included their parents. They said that it was all very well the school having an anti-racist policy that was read out in assembly after an incident had occurred, but what they needed was education about why various groups of people have come to this country and why they have a right to be here. The group concluded that if attitudes were to change, the issues of race and anti-racism must be part of the timetable, not just a policy document or a reaction to an incident.   (Researcher's notes)

These comments by students were made during the stage of the process when researchers were meeting with groups of representatives from each year. Each year group met on three occasions. Using case study material and other age-appropriate exercises, groups discussed problems of, and their preferred solutions to, bullying and violence in the school. In parallel with this, similar problem-solving sessions with staff were taking place. At the end of this process, a staff/student victimisation working party was established, its job being to operationalise policies and strategies adopted by students and staff . The extracts from the minutes of the staff/student victimisation working party in the box below, give the flavour of the discussion and some of the measures instituted to reduce violent victimisation.

Extracts from the minutes of the staff/student victimisation working party at the London secondary school

Public apologies

It was felt that it would usually be better to confront somebody in front of the class rather than the whole school, although it was important that the whole school knew who the persistent bullies were.

It was felt that 'mediation', an opportunity for the two people involved to talk it out with the help of a teacher, was a good idea if both people were willing. This would need to be discussed by staff and could involve some training sessions for staff who are to be involved.

Behavioural policy

It was felt that few students actually knew what the school policy, school rules and students' rights and responsibilities were. It was felt that not all staff knew them either, *or how they should respond to an infringement of them.*

It was agreed that there should be a School Policy Study Morning on violence after Easter for years 7/8/9 when years 10/11 were on 'work experience'. Students could use role play or video to bring issues alive and Mr Smith agreed to get Bullying videos. Anti-racism and anti-sexism policies would also be considered during the Study Morning.

Racist and sexist violence and intimidation

It was felt that racism and sexism occupied a more central place in the curriculum three years ago when the staff working parties on these issues were still meeting. There is less 'permeation' now partly because of shortage of time, but also perhaps because these working parties are no longer there to keep the issues at the forefront. It was felt that as a result, anti-racist and anti-sexist policies in the school seem to have gone into abeyance. There was a suggestion that the decline in the enforcement of anti-racist and anti-sexist policies had contributed to the school feeling less safe than it used to.

It was agreed that student/staff anti-racist and anti-sexist working parties should be convened and should meet regularly to discuss whether the policies are working and how they can be made to work better.

It was felt that although PSE was used to raise these issues it was often difficult for individuals to express what they felt, particularly if the person victimising or intimidating them was in the same class.

The working party felt that there was not enough time for trusting relationships to be made between form teachers and their students. It was agreed that if form teachers were able to take their own form for PSE and use it to discuss issues affecting them this would be better. Longer registration periods in which informal discussions could take place would also help students to feel less isolated and vulnerable. It might be that one period a week could be devoted to 'form time', or school could finish a bit earlier one day so that students with something on their minds could discuss it with their form teacher or any other teacher that they felt would listen to them.

Were this to happen, it would be very important that all students and staff knew about the procedures for dealing with information about victimisation and that the staff implemented them. There was also an important question to be sorted out about what information was confidential and what was not.

There are a number of issues here which will have to be taken to the Head, the Governors and the Staff Group for a decision.

It was agreed that as part of the school's anti-sexist commitment, mixed sports teams should be available to girls who want them; they should not have to ask. It was agreed that a 50/50 Mixed Team Tutor Group Tournament could be organised as part of the programme of lunchtime activities.

Lunchtime activities

It was agreed that a programme of lunchtime activities would help to reduce victimisation. There was some concern, however, that if older students were given responsibility for organising them, they might abuse their authority and start to bully younger students. It was agreed that they should work under the supervision of a teacher and that only selected volunteers who did it in order to gain accredited youth work or play leadership experience, and whose work would be evaluated, in part, by 'consumers', should be able to do this. Activities planned included a Chess Club, Homework Club, Staffed Year Bases and Tournaments. In response to earlier requests the school was making available a room to Bangladeshi girls who wanted to use it at playtimes. It was agreed that any shortage of adults or particular skills could be made good by approaching the Local Age Concern branch or Trades Unions which are in touch with skilled and experienced people who are currently unemployed.

It was agreed that the other side of this initiative was to ensure that the teachers and meals supervisors in the playground were looking out for victimisation and felt willing and supported to intervene. Staff and ancillary workers therefore need time to read and discuss the policy and procedures for dealing with it.

Responses to victimised students

It was recognised that when staff were under pressure, and even though they usually believed what they were told, it was very easy to let allegations of victimisation drift and not to follow the agreed procedures. It was hoped that the School Policy Study Morning would reinforce the need to 'follow through' on these complaints.

It was agreed that a 'Bully Box' should be constructed so that pupils who are being victimised or intimidated can meet with the teacher of their choice to discuss the problem in confidence. By regularly collecting the forms staff/students can monitor patterns, and the extent, of bullying in the school and get some idea about whether their other initiatives are having an effect.

It was also felt that some of the older students who had had problems in the school when they were younger, could offer some younger students continuing help and support and that staff might want to suggest this to some of the younger students if they think it appropriate.

Penalties for violent aggression

It was felt that fixed-term exclusion would only work if the excluded student had to complete a violence-focussed work book during their exclusion. It was felt that any further incidents after this should be dealt with by some kind of community service – putting something back into the school. This could include cleaning up the play areas after school. It also makes sense to keep back after school a person who has victimised somebody, so that the victimised student is not worried about being bothered again on their way home.

Following the launch of these, and the other strategies devised by the group, the incidence of reported victimisation notified via the Bully Box rocketed. It was as if the combined impact of these strategies, all of which grew out of a protracted process of consultation had lifted the lid of a Pandora's box of victimisation. Interestingly, once the new climate of openness was established, reports of bullying via the Bully Box declined a little, whereas face-to-face reports to, and discussions with staff increased markedly:

The children come and talk to us far more easily, not just about bullying, although that's important, but about all sorts of other things that are happening in and around the school. I

think the victimisation project has really got us talking to each other and it's not always easy for us to hear some of the things the children want to say, but it must be better than before.
                                                                                    (Year 11 teacher)

Given the energy and commitment that both students and staff had invested in the project it was both surprising and disappointing that the returns from the questionnaire surveys showed little apparent change in the levels of violent victimisation over the period.

On the face of it, it appears that the initiative in the London secondary school made little impact on levels of victimisation. However, there are a number of factors which must be taken into account in order to set these findings in context. The period in which the initiative was undertaken coincided with a marked increase in the proportion of Bangladeshi students entering the school and in racial tension in the area, which culminated in the election of a British National Party candidate in the adjacent Isle of Dogs ward. It was clear that the racial tension and hostility within the school and the neighbourhood was attributable in part, at least, to the heightened profile given to race and ethnicity in the protracted and acrimonious run-up to this election. Thus, during this period there was an escalation of violent inter-racial conflict in the immediate neighbourhood some of which involved students from the school. Given these circumstances, the fact that the incidence of violent victimisation was reduced only very slightly might be interpreted as positive. Nonetheless there was a modest decrease in the percentage of students who suffered the most serious forms of victimisation from 17 to 14 per cent and more remarkably, the numbers of youngsters reporting racist name calling dropped from 23 to 18 per cent. Threats with weapons were down falling from five per cent to three per cent and those being 'touched up' from 12 to 8 per cent.

These reductions are not statistically significant but, more encouragingly, if we isolate Year 7 students, we find that the most recent cohort entering the school at the end of the action-research period had to endure significantly less physical violence than their predecessors. In the first questionnaire 33 per cent of Year 7 students reported having been 'hit or kicked', whereas in the latter questionnaire this figure was reduced to 18 per cent. In its work in the London secondary school, the research team devoted considerable energy to the plight of the youngest and most vulnerable students, and they were closely involved in the project. In a subsequent study it emerged that when this cohort of students entered year eight, their levels of victimisation were far lower than expected, suggesting that the initiative may have had a differential impact upon different years of students.

The testimony of those involved in the life of the school suggests that these changes have contributed to altered perceptions of the level of threat and anxiety in the school.

The kids are more friendly to each other, there's less bullying. You don't see people getting beaten up – or complaining of having been beaten up.   (Year 10 student)

It's been a lot of hard work, but it's been worth it because we've seen the changes and the improvement.   (Year 11 student (member of staff-student anti-bullying working party))

There has been a clear change in students' attitudes, the most important being that they would report incidents of bullying. In the past they thought it wasn't worthwhile. There is more trust between students and staff.   (Deputy head)

The ethos of the school has improved . . . *The atmosphere is noticeably calmer; students'*
attitudes towards one another appear *much more* positive *with a significant reduction in overt*
racial tension and sexism.   (Extract from HMI report on the school)

Conclusion

The initiative did not aim to prescribe a 'quick fix'. The target of the intervention was the
organisational culture of the schools. The intention was to create the conditions for, and to set in
train, change in those organisational cultures. The strategies employed to this end varied from
school to school because each school had a different culture, confronted different problems and,
in consequence, opted for different 'solutions'. In all four cases, however, a protracted and
extensive consultative stage preceded the choice of a 'solution'. This process, of itself, was
probably as significant in its impact upon school culture as the solutions that were eventually
selected.

It is evident that the initiative had a significant impact upon the primary schools involved in the
project. On Merseyside, participants chose to utilise a child-centred peer education programme
and in London the choice was for brief focused work with teaching and ancillary staff and a
video dramatisation of the school's behaviour policy. As we have already noted, in the London
school the reduction in victimisation appears to be related to an increased willingness of teaching
and ancillary staff to intervene in incidents; whereas in the Merseyside primary school the
changes appear to be related to the increased confidence of students to report victimisation. In
both cases, improvements appear to hinge on the development of a shared perception by adults
and children of those behaviours which can be tolerated, and those which cannot. For this to
happen, communication between people at different levels in the organisation is essential.

In the Merseyside secondary school this process was achieved through the means of curriculum
content which drew upon the lived experience of the children and in the London secondary school,
communication was improved by engaging all students in a process of democratic decision-
making. Our experience also suggests that simultaneous changes in both the physical and social
environments of a school is necessary if individual and group behaviour is to change significantly.

References

Dennington, J. and Pitts, J. (1991) *Developing Services for Young People in Crisis.* Longman.
Downes, D. (1990) *Public Violence on Two Estates.* Home Office (Unpublished).
Farrington, D. and West, D. (1993) Criminal, Penal and Life Histories of Chronic Offenders: Risk
    and Protective Factors and Early Identification. *Criminal Behaviour and Mental Health.* 3,
    492-523.
Graham, J. (1988) *Schools, Disruptive Behaviour and Delinquency,* Home Office Research Study
    No.96. Home Office.
Hargreaves, D. (1967) *Social Relations in the Secondary School.* Routledge and Kegan Paul.
Jones, M. (1968) *The Therapeutic Community.* Penguin.
Mathiesen, T. (1964) *The Defences of the Weak.* Tavistock.
Millham, S., Bullock, R. and Cherret, P. (1975) *After Grace: Teeth: A Comparative Study of the
    Experience of Boys in Approved Schools.* Human Context Books.

Millham, S., Bullock, R. and Hosie, K. (1978) *Locking up Children: Secure Provision Within the Child Care System*. Saxon House.

Olweus, D. (1989) Bully/Victim Problems Amongst School Children: Basic Facts and the Effects of a School-Based Intervention Programme, in Robin, K. and Pepler, D. (Eds.) *The Development and Treatment of Childhood Aggression*. Enbaum.

Pitts, J. (1993) Developing School and Community Links to Prevent Bullying, in Tattum, D. (Ed.) *Understanding and Managing Bullying*. Heinemann.

Pitts, J. and Smith, P. (1995) *Preventing School Bullying*. Home Office.

Power, M. J., Benn, R. T. and Norris, J. N. (1972) Neighbourhood, School and Juveniles Before the Courts. *British Journal of Criminology*. 12: 111-32.

Robbins, D. (1989) *Child Care Policy: Putting It In Writing*. II/4SC.

Rutter, M., Maughan, B., Mortimore, P., Ouston, J. and Smith, A. (1979) *Fifteen Thousand Hours*. Harvard University Press.

Rutter, M. and Maughan, B. (1987) Pupils Progress in Selective and Non-selective Schools. *School Organisation*. 7:1 Jan. 50–68.

Annexe

John Pitts and the editors would like to thank the Home Office and the Police Research Group for permission to reprint the following practical material which was included by John Pitts and Philip Smith in their work with the schools in London and Merseyside.

It is derived from: Sections 2, 4, 7, 9 and 10 of *Preventing School Bullying* (1995) by John Pitts and Philip Smith. It was published by the Police Research Group, Crime Detection and Prevention Series Paper No. 63.

Initial staff consultation exercise
Sheet A. Break time

It is break time. You are walking in the playground. A fifteen year old boy hits a twelve year old boy very hard, pushes him to the floor and shouts abuse at him. The twelve year old is crying.

What will you say to the fifteen year old?

What will you say to the twelve year old?

What will you do then?

What information will you need?

If your answer to any of these questions is 'it depends', what does it depend on?

The following day you learn from a number of your pupils that the fifteen year old attacked the twelve year old outside his block of flats that same evening. What do you do?

Sheet B. Who does what?

If the fifteen year old described on sheet A were to continue to bully younger students, what action do you think the following people should take (please be as specific as you can):

1. Form teachers

2. Year heads

3. Deputy heads

4. The head

5. The parents of the bullying pupil

6. The parents of the bullied pupils

7. The school governors?

8. The local education authority?

Sheet C. Sanctions and restrictions

Research indicates that while many students are involved in bullying from time to time, some will persist in this behaviour.

Suggest the penalties or remedies you would consider appropriate in the case of a child who bullies the same younger student three more times after an initial warning.

	Penalty	Remedy
1st. Time:		
2nd. Time:		
3rd. Time:		

Sheet D. Surveillance and diversion

Suggest in two minutes:

1. As many practical ways as you can in which bullying in the playground could be observed more easily.

2. Practical ways in which breaktimes could be made more interesting.

3. Practical ways in which the journey to and from school could be made safer.

Initial secondary school student exercise
Break time

(note the ages of the members of your group) (. . .)

A fifteen year old boy is punching a thirteen year old boy and shouting at him. The thirteen year old is very frightened and upset but the fifteen year old keeps on hitting him and shouting.

What do you think the other students who are watching this should do?

What do you think you should do?

What do you think the member of staff on duty should do?

What do you think the head or deputy head should do?

What if it continues?

If the fifteen year old is warned but does it again to the same boy the following week what should happen to him?

Who should take the decisions about what happens to the fifteen year old? Think about the good and bad things about these alternatives.

1. the head or deputy?

2. the class teacher

3. other members of the boy's own class?

4. people from other classes who don't know the boy who was bullied?

5. the boy who was bullied?

What should happen if the fifteen year old kept on bullying people despite what was done?

Being bullied

If you were being bullied, when and where would you be most in danger?

If you were being bullied, what kind of help would you need?

How could the following people best help you?

1. Members of your class?
2. Members of other classes?
3. The teacher on duty?
4. Your class teacher?
5. The head or deputy head?

What could stop you?

If you were bullying somebody, what could you be promised that might make you stop doing it?

If you were bullying somebody, what sort of threat might make you stop doing it?

If you were bullying somebody, who could you talk to if you were worried about it?

The Merseyside Secondary School Personal Empowerment Programme (Developed as an eight-session module for the personal and social education curriculum)

Week 1. Communication

Introductions:	Who are we? What are our hopes and fears for these sessions? (participants form pairs to identify apprehensions and expectations)
	Group Leader draws these issues together and identifies shared and different objectives which participants wish to pursue.
Brainstorm:	Ground Rules for Working Together:
	Who talks when?
	Interpersonal behaviour
	Language/Communication
Getting to know you 1:	(Communication Exercises):
	Students find somebody in the group they don't know very well and find out as much as they can about them in five minutes. Pairs return to large group and each introduces their partner to the other members.
Getting to know you 2:	(Blocks to Communication):
	What is difficult about getting to know people? 'they won't like me', 'I won't like them', 'they won't listen to me'.
Round up:	Go round the group saying, in turn, what you understand about getting to know people that you didn't understand before.

Week 2. Active listening

Teachers remind students about the purpose of the sessions and the ground rules agreed in the previous session.

Game, fruit salad:	(Listening Exercise):
	All group members sit in a circle and are given the name of a fruit – apple, orange or pear. When the person in the middle calls, for example, 'apple' all the 'apples' have to run round the outside of the cicle. When the central person calls 'fruit salad' everybody has to.
Brainstorm:	Go round the group and ask how do we know when people are listening to us? How do we know when they are not? What stops people listening? . . . they're in a hurry, not interested, too noisy themselves, tired, distracted, believe they know what we are about to say etc.
3 × 3 (Exercise):	Group divides up into groups of three and one person talks about something they are very interested in for three minutes.

One person is instructed to listen carefully for the first minute and then stop listening and the third person is an observer who gives feedback on what happened . . . body language, strategies for regaining peoples' interest etc etc.

Round up: Discuss what group members are going to do in the forthcoming week to improve their listening skills. They are asked to think of somebody they don't always listen to and to think what they can do about it.

Week 3. Improving perception

Teachers remind students about the purpose of the sessions and the ground rules agreed in the first session.

Old person young person: (Exercise):

The group divides up into pairs, one taking the part of a young person and one of an old person and talk about what they would expect one another to be like.

Whole group de-brief on the assumptions people brought to bear.

First impression: (Brainstorm):

What do we notice when we first meet people? How is this shaped by age, race and gender? What effects do our initial perceptions have on our subsequent behaviour? Do we get to know them, like or dislike them, ignore, admire or fear them?

Pictures (Exercise):   Group divides up into fours and each four is handed some pictures of people where it is not obvious what they are doing. The group is asked to think of as many different accounts of events as possible and to make explicit the different sorts of assumptions which led to the different interpretations.

Round up: Go round the group asking what are the dangers of judging by first appearances.

Week 4. Aggression or assertion?

Teachers remind students about the purpose of the sessions and the ground rules agreed in the first session. They add: 'So far we have looked at getting to know one another, listening to each other and the dangers of judging by first appearance. Now we are going to consider how we get along with people in a variety of situations. Sometimes people feel happy, sad, angry or uncertain'.

Making choices: Introduction to whole group 'Your best friend wants you to do something you don't want to do (e.g. bunk off school, lend them your pocket money; take drugs, pinch a car). How do you handle it?'

Brainstorm:	'What can you do?' Teachers group responses under *passive*, *aggressive* and *assertive* and ask group to think about the choices they have.
Role play:	In 3s, two volunteers to play parts of best friends who disagree on a course of action and the strategies they use. Third person acts as observer and reports back to large group. Role players feedback about whether, as best friends, they were able to persuade the other or not and whether they felt able to say yes or no when under pressure. Teachers highlight differences between aggressive and assertive behaviour.
Round up:	Ask group members to identify a situation in which it felt good to say no.

Week 5. Building self-esteem

Teachers remind students about the purpose of the sessions and the ground rules agreed in the first session.

My personal shield:	How I defend myself against being hurt. Group members are handed a blank sheet of paper and asked to write down what their shield is. Papers put into a hat and mixed up. Group members take one out of the hat in turn and read them out. All group members who use that strategy are asked to put their hand up. Teachers discusses the importance of our shields and that we use them to keep feeling OK about ourselves when bad things happen to use or are said about us. Group is asked to identify situations in which one's self-esteem can be damaged.
My personal mallet:	How I put myself down and deny that I am OK and that there are things that I am good at. Group divides up into pairs and each member tells the other what they think is good about them.

Week 6. Building confidence

Teachers remind students about the purpose of the sessions and the ground rules areed in the first session.

Warm-up:	Fruit salad (c.f. week 2.)
Brainstorm:	What sort of situations make you feel unconfident: knowing or not knowing your school, people being nasty to you, when you are frightened, when you have to ask for something from someone who appears to be more confident and powerful than you.

Exercise:	Half the class walks around the room in a confident manner. Half the class walks around the room in an unconfident manner. Teachers ask group what it looks like and what it feels like.
Brainstorm:	What do confident people look like? What do people who lack confidence look like? Teachers ask 'what is the difference between confidence and aggression?' ('I feel good and you're OK' versus 'I feel good because I'm making you feel awful')
Round up:	How I will try to be more confident in the coming week.

Week 7. Working together

Teachers remind students about the purpose of the sessions and the ground rules agreed in the first session.

Brainstorm:	Name all the teams you can think of (not just football teams). What are the differences between a 'good' team and a 'bad' team. Teachers group responses under *co-operation* and *collaboration*.
Brainstorm:	What are the benefits of working together instead of alone: more fun; more ideas; can take on more difficult and interesting tasks; complementary skills and knowledge.
Exercise:	In teams of six, group members use newspaper, cardboard, straws etc. to make any object they like.
De-brief:	Groups are asked to think and talk about how working together enhanced the task and some of the difficulties, or things that you have to take into account when collaborating with other people.
Round up:	Go round the group saying, in turn, what you understand about working together that you didn't understand before.

Week 8. Summing up

Teachers remind students about the purpose of the sessions and the ground rules agreed in the first session. They say that this sessions aims to pull together all the learning that has gone on in the previous seven weeks.

Week 1. Communication
Week 2. Active listening
Week 3. Improving perception
Week 4. Aggression or assertion
Week 5. Building self-esteem

Week 6. Building confidence
Week 7. Working together
Teachers ask group to divide into seven smaller groups and spend 15 minutes identifying the three most important points that we should remember from each of these sessions and one 'unanswered question' (on flip-chart paper).

The 21 most important points are then bluetacked to the walls and clarification sought and offered.

The seven questions are then put to the whole group as a basis for discussion and revision.

Round up: All group members, in turn, have an opportunity to bid farewell to the group and offer it a gift in the form of some words of advice or encouragement.

Bully box forms
Form for students

Bullying

You have a right to be safe and happy at this school and if you are not we want to hear about it. Just fill in this form and put it through the letter box in your year room.

The teacher you have named will send you back the tear-off slip at the bottom of this form telling you when and where you can meet them.

Name . . . .

Form . . . .

Teacher you wish to speak with . . . .

✂ ————————————————————————

Staff reply slip

Dear . . . .

Thank you for your note. I would like to meet you at (time) . . . .

at . . . . (place) to talk about it.

Yours. . . . .

Victimisation monitoring sheet
Staff monitoring slip

Student's form No. . . . .   Race . . . .   M/F . . . .

Names of alleged perpetrators . . . .
. . . .
. . . .

What form did the reported bullying take?   Tick if appropriate

Name calling or isolation because of race, colour or culture   ☐

Name calling or isolation because of sex or gender   ☐

Name calling or isolation because of family   ☐

Name calling or isolation because of something else. Please specify   ☐

Threats   ☐

Threats with a weapon   ☐

Threats and theft of property   ☐

Property stolen or damaged   ☐

Physical violence   ☐

Physical violence with a weapon   ☐

Sexual molestation or assault   ☐

Other. Please specify . . . .
. . . .

What action did you take?
. . . .

Name . . . .   Date . . . .

CHAPTER 11

Working with violent men in institutions and the community

Alison Skinner and Gwyneth Boswell

Introduction

The over-representation of men as offenders in institutions and community-based programmes has been neglected as a topic in the study of crime for a considerable period. However, over the last decade, researchers and practitioners have begun to pay more attention to methods of addressing the root causes of violence and crime in ways that make sense to the experiences of individual men.

Research with young men, conducted over a long period, has examined the characteristics of boys who later committed violent offences. Farrington (1989) concluded that for children between the ages of eight and ten, the best predictors of future violent behaviour included physical neglect, harsh and erratic discipline from parents and separation because of parental conflict. Other contributing factors included low family income, large family size and a parent with a criminal conviction. More specifically, a New York State study found that males who were the victims of physical punishment at age eight tended to commit violent offences up to the age of 30 (Eron, Huesmann and Zelli, 1991). An important study by Widom also focused specifically upon the relationship between child abuse and neglect and later violent criminal behaviour (Widom, 1989). The latter identified a large sample of children who had been victims of confirmed cases of child abuse and neglect 20 years before and established a matched control group of non-abused children. She then determined the extent to which each group had engaged in officially recorded delinquent and adult behaviour of a criminal or violent criminal nature.

The study produced a prediction that, 'early childhood victimisation (i.e. abuse and neglect) has demonstrable long-term consequences for delinquency, adult criminality and violent criminal behaviour.' In particular it found that physical abuse in childhood led significantly to later criminal behaviour, when other factors such as age, sex and race were held constant.

Groupwork programmes with male offenders are becoming increasingly commonplace. These often explore the factors in relationships and other personal encounters in everyday life that can spark a violent reaction from men. Others take masculinity itself as a subject and enable groups of men to share with each other their experiences of growing up, and learning how to act like a man, and examine commonly held assumptions. This work may either take place in prison with groups of offenders on long-term or short-term sentences, or in probation day centres. A number of different programmes, mainly run by the probation service, have been reported in the literature.

The books by Newburn and Mair (1996) *Working with Men* and *Good Practice in Working with Violence* by Kemshall and Pritchard (1999) also contain a collection of chapters in which various groupwork programmes of this kind are described.

Working on masculinity issues

Work with men on issues around masculinity has had a relatively short pedigree in the social work and criminal justice field, although the issue emerged much earlier in the youth work field in response to the growing movement of work with girls and young women (Lloyd, 1996).

Mark Johnstone (2000) asserts that the probation service:

> . . . has not consistently and explicitly encouraged integration of theoretical understandings of the social construction of masculinity into work with male offenders generally. There have been some notable exceptions, where men's offending programmes have focused on the link between masculinity and offending, but too often these have been due to the commitment of key individuals, rather than policy-led practice response.   (Johnstone, 2000)

He notes that gender-related work with men could be categorised in two broad, overlapping theoretical standpoints:

1. Personal development initiatives which critically evaluate stereotypical roles and promote diversity of beliefs, thought, action and identity. This explores male socialisation in an attempt to induce an assertive and responsible approach rather than one governed by dominant social norms and expectation.
2. Power relations and in particular, male abuse of power. This perspective is used when working with men who have victimised women and children.

He suggests that work with men subject to the probation service should aim to introduce critical, alternate and creative thinking processes by exploring the social construction of masculinity. Since this will involve changes to long-established patterns of thinking and behaviour he identifies three key stages to the process. These are as follows:

- An awareness stage that seeks to introduce contemplation, exploration and discussion of the social construction of masculinity and the links with criminal behaviour.
- A deconstructing stage that seeks to break down the social construction of masculinity and explores the underpinning beliefs and behaviours.
- The reframing stage which attempts to promote and construct alternative beliefs and behaviours.

Murphy (1996) describes a group on the theme of men and offending run by the Camberwell Probation Centre. This is a 12-session programme with compulsory attendance.

The essence of it is an examination of masculine socialisation in terms of establishing a pecking order, finding a role, belonging and taking part in group activities.

The programme covers the following elements:

1. Introduction, aims, ground rules, roles of leaders.
2. Expectations of men, public heroes, private heroes (types of people respected).
3. 'When did I become a man?' Transition process: 'proving' to self and others.
4. Transition process: dependent-interdependent roles in teenage groups.

5. 'Ways men learn to cope' in school, prison. Tensions between public actions and private thoughts and feelings.
6. Male image photopack. Exercises dealing with male power, identity and feelings.
7. Benefits of offending.
8. Costs of offending.
9. Impact of social class on men.
10. Challenging racism.
11. Challenging sexism.
12. Review of group and evaluation.

Sessions one to six are the essential building blocks in the process of reflection, others can be developed to address specific themes such as anger, violence, drug or alcohol use, health, parenting, use of time, change, sexuality, homophobia and relationships according to the needs of a particular group.

Anger management work with offenders

Gardiner and Nesbit (1996) describe a cognitive behavioural groupwork model with male offenders run by the Newcastle upon Tyne Intensive Probation Unit. Making attendance voluntary was an important aspect from their point of view as they believed it attracted a more motivated clientele and improved, rather than diminished attendance levels. Courses were held on neutral territory in the city centre, close to bus routes, as it was thought that attendance at the local NHS drugs facility could be seen as stigmatising.

These courses were run full-time over three to five consecutive days, rather than one short session per week. It was argued that this would enable the groups to form more readily. Considerable attention was paid to ensuring that the methods used made the course accessible to the men taking part.

The authors noted that many offenders did not have successful school careers, and flipchart and pen methods of groupwork can be reminiscent of the classroom. Alternatives they suggested included:

> . . . viewing and discussing pre-recorded tapes, collage work where offenders cut up magazines and create their own composite picture on a given theme, small groupwork, role play and drama. Rather than drawing a strip cartoon of a particular offence, course members may be asked to act it out, positioning other members and freezing the various themes. If this can be recorded with a Polaroid camera, a story board can be built up.
>
> (Gardiner and Nesbit, 1996)

Keeping your head is the Unit's anger management course for male offenders and is a four-day course. Abusive language and behaviour, alcohol misuse and drug taking are banned and group members share their expectations. The group brainstorms their beliefs about aggression and violence; when it is appropriate to hit out and against whom.

They also do an exercise called *5WH*. This is used to analyse incidents or offences. Members analyse a real event from their experience in terms of who, what, where, when, why and how, reliving the progression towards the offence. The trainers use a 'time-out' mechanism during the day to avoid the build-up of tension and frustration.

Other exercises explore techniques of negotiation and anger control. Members brainstorm situations in which negotiation usually takes place and try to identify behavioural factors that support successful negotiation. Anger control is considered by the authors as a central strategy to any attempt to deal with problems of aggression and violence. Group members identify things that tend to provoke them and any successful avoidance strategies they have adopted. Factors, which are built into the programme from the start, are:

- a high ratio of course leaders to participants
- use of community-based venues
- insistence on high quality materials
- time for evaluation and development

Morrison (1997) planned some anger control work with a transient and unpredictable population of short sentence and remanded prisoners. The programme took the following form:

- Introductions and issues.
- Diaries: members kept anger diaries over a week.
- Thematic exercises: cognitive and behaviour based exercises and role plays etc.
- Stress management: mainly featuring relaxation exercises.
- Risk assessment: included instruction on the meaning of risk (via brainstorming).
- Assertiveness training.
- Power and control theme.
- Feelings.
- Attitudes and beliefs.
- Victim awareness.
- Final comments.

The sessions ran for 75 minutes for a group numbering 25–30 in total. This is a relatively large group and experienced groupworkers advocate 10–12 at a time as an optimal number.

The programme was designed to give participants the opportunity to gain insights into their offence behaviours, as well as strategies for modifying those behaviours, with both elements being present in each session. This provided greater equality of opportunity for remand and short-term prisoners who are often excluded from this type of programme. Weekly feedback from prisoners described, in a significant number of cases, increased control, heightened insights and day-to-day application of the techniques and concepts communicated.

Courtney and Hodgkinson (1999) developed the IDEA (It Depends Evaluation Analysis) model because participants attending their probation day centre had difficulty in 'making sense' of a violent offence because 'it depended' on so many variables.

The initial starting point was to examine the thought processes and perceived pressures which participants considered underpinned the decision to use violence.

They developed exercises to focus more closely on which type of people or specific persons were most or least at risk of violence perpetrated by group members. These included a continuum rating exercise and various role play scenarios, in which features of the potential target such as gender, age, race, relationship, sexuality and status were changed, allowing participants to see that their reactions to different people would result in different outcomes. Participants were asked to record information about the people who were most or least at risk from them in a conflict situation.

Group members were also asked to identify environmental factors that contributed to them getting into trouble. This revealed patterns such as the frequency of fights occurring in or around fast food outlets, taxi ranks or neighbours' houses. The notion of safe places was also explored.

Participants identified the characteristics of high risk areas, variations in such factors as space, lighting, sound levels, together with action, tension and numbers of people present. Some participants felt compelled to use violence to satisfy a sense of social obligation to their peer group and themselves. Collective examination of these informal rules can be done via role-play scenarios, in which the audience to an incident is systematically changed, or debates which require the arguing of two conflicting points of view.

Participants were given a reminder of their life history and a consideration of the factors that had shaped their attitudes so far. Issues of morality and conscience were raised and considered between group members. To hear fellow group members expressing doubt or disapproval about firmly held beliefs had great impact.

Individual expectations of the end result of their actions are another factor in the decision to use violence. Exercises were used that focused participants on the overall gains and losses of violence, particularly the cost to both direct and indirect victims.

By asking participants to consider each of these elements, by identifying high and low risks and their own strengths and weaknesses, it was found that individuals had assembled the mental tools necessary to bring about real change. The authors found that if people were able to make progress in several areas, a stronger sense of self-control started to replace impulsive behaviour.

Experiences of abuse and loss in the Section 53 population

During the course of a study of the custodial experiences and needs of Section 53 offenders (Boswell, 1991) it was found that 50 per cent of the offender sample had a background of some kind of child abuse (i.e. physical, sexual, emotional, organised ritual or a combination of all of them). There was also an apparent prevalence of bereavement and other significant loss experiences. These offenders are children and young people aged from ten to seventeen, who commit grave crimes involving violence or intended violence and are sentenced to be detained, some indeterminately, under Section 53 of the Children and Young Persons Act 1933.

Table 1. Emotional, sexual, physical and organised or ritual abuse (n = 200)

Experience of emotional abuse	28.5%
Experience of sexual abuse	29.0%
Experience of physical abuse	40.0%
Organised or ritual abuse	1.5%
Combination of two or more	27.0%

In a further study, (Boswell, 1995) 200 files representing 78 adult prisoners, 59 inmates of Youth Offender Institution and 63 Department of Health residents were scrutinised. The ages of those studied ranged from 14–59. The five main categories studied were those of emotional, sexual, physical abuse, organised or ritual abuse, and loss. The following results were obtained.

In all, 72 per cent of the total sample had experienced emotional, sexual, physical abuse, or organised or ritual abuse, or combinations of these categories. In addition, 57 per cent had experienced significant loss via bereavement, ending of contact with a significant adult or both. There is little doubt that child abuse and the experience of significant loss, when no mediating factor, (such as good educational experience, or a listening, responsible adult) is present constitutes unresolved trauma that will manifest itself in some way at a later date.

These findings highlight the importance of examining further the links between those young people who end up in residential or custodial settings because of their violence (whether criminalised or not) and the background factors in their lives.

It is particularly important that staff are trained and encouraged to respond to examples of acting-out behaviour by disturbed young people in a way that seeks first to understand and second to react, though it is acknowledged that the reaction often has to follow very closely after the process of 'making sense' of behaviour.

Incarcerated young people who have committed violent acts and offences need clear information about their legal rights and their expected custodial career progression. They also need continuity of education, through-care and offence-focused work. Particular attention should be paid to the possibility of trauma in their earlier lives and counselling provided to help them work constructively through this.

Managing violence

Stanton-Greenwood (1999) discussed techniques for managing violence in residential settings. She notes that there are factors peculiar to residential settings that can intensify the propensity for and severity of violence. There is the possibility that residential care workers and their clients may not be able to leave potentially violent situations, they form a captive audience of victims amongst peers and staff, and there can also be a group effect in violence or unrest, where one client can affect the stability of others.

Research (quoted by Stanton-Greenwood (1999)) carried out by McDonnell (1992) in 39 children's residential settings shows eleven main causes of challenging behaviour:
1. Being unable to communicate a need other than through challenging behaviour.
2. Being confused through inconsistent staff requests.
3. Medical problems.
4. Inactivity. Boredom and the time to worry about problems can trigger violence.
5. Demands and requests made or refused by the staff.
6. Changes and inconsistency in routines.
7. Environmental effects:
    (a) lack of personal space
    (b) excessive heat
    (c) excessive noise
    (d) seating, lighting, décor problems
8. Relationship problems.
9. Early childhood traumas.

10. Being provoked or wound up.
11. Being bullied.   (Stanton-Greenwood, 1999)

Risk assessment can be deployed to analyse and assess the severity and frequency of risk, likelihood of violence and potential hazards, in any given activity, with a given client, in a given environment.

Stanton-Greenwood (1999) sets out certain principles of good practice, which may help to de-escalate a potentially violent situation:
1. Know your client, their background, triggers and individual pathways to violence.
2. Know yourself and your own triggers. Fear can be confused with anger.
3. Avoid confrontation:
   • have a calm manner
   • beware of body movements and position
   • do not corner your client
4. Avoid physical contact and keep your distance.
5. Avoid the phrase 'because I say so': talk of house rules instead.
6. Do not include other issues and pile on the agony.
7. Do not make an ultimatum you cannot keep.
8. Assess the situation. Ask yourself the questions:
   • what am I feeling right now?
   • what does this person need or want?
   • what is going on in the group right now?

She further suggests that cycles of behaviour, and successful or unsuccessful interventions, are recorded so that others may learn from this and clients are not constantly practised on.

Another useful set of practical materials for developing a groupwork programme to work with young people who act 'oppressively' is contained in *Time to Grow* (Chapman, 2000). Through his work in Northern Ireland, Chapman developed a set of processes aimed at challenging young people and confronting their prejudices. Towards the end of the Workbook section, he offers a set of questions and activities around the theme of citizenship, which a group worker can use to engage young people in discussion about their behaviour. Among them are:
• *How do people abuse power?* Have a dialogue on power issues e.g. violence, exploitation, abuse, poverty, discrimination, exclusion, intimidation, coercion etc.
• *Can you remember an incident when someone had power over you and you were powerless?* Through dialogue, explore examples and feelings at the time and how the incident may continue to affect the person.
• *Can you remember an incident when you had power over someone who felt powerless?* Through dialogue, explore examples and feelings at the time and how the incident may continue to affect the participant and the other person. Consider how the other person might have felt? Does oppressing someone else also have a negative effect upon the oppressor?
• *Have you ever stood up to someone who had power over you?* Explore examples and consider what qualities and support one needs.
• *Have you ever used power justly?* Explore examples and consider what constitutes the just use of power.

- *Developing a sense of responsibility for others?* Ask the group to pick a disadvantaged group whom they would like to learn more about and support in some way. Identify a charity that works on behalf of this group and invite or visit a representative. Seek to understand the needs and problems of the group and consider what individuals could do to help. Disability awareness training is a particularly effective means of achieving this objective.

Conclusions

Analysis of the previous evidence indicates that violent behaviour by both young and older men has root causes and underlying patterns that can be addressed by group programmes of various kinds. In these programmes it will often be necessary to examine the social construction of a version of masculinity, that seeks to maintain its integrity through threats and violence towards other men and female partners. The literature demonstrates however that there are now exercises and approaches that can help men rethink their behaviour in different settings, which can be supportive, rather than confrontational.

References

Boswell, G. (1991) *Waiting for Change: An Exploration of the Experiences and Needs of Section 53 Offenders*. The Prince's Trust.

Boswell, G. (1995) *Violent Victims: The Prevalence of Abuse and Loss in the Lives of Section 53 Offenders*. The Prince's Trust.

Chapman, T. (2000) *Time to Grow: A Comprehensive Programme for People Working with Young Offenders and Young People at Risk*. Russell House Publishing.

Courtney, J. and Hodgkinson, I. (1999) Practice Note: The 'IDEA' Approach to Groupwork with Violent Offenders. *Probation Journal*. 46: 3, Sept. 192–4.

Dobash, R. (2000) Domestic Violence Programmes: A Framework for Change. *Probation Journal*. 47:1, Mar. 18–29.

Eron, L.D., Huesmann, L.R. and Zelli, A. (1991) The Role of Parental Variables in the Learning of Aggression, in Pepler, D.J. and Rubin, K.H. (Eds.) *The Development and Treatment of Childhood Aggression*. Lawrence Erlbaum.

Farrington, D.P. (1989) Early Predictors of Adolescent Aggression and Adult Violence. *Violence and Victims*. 4: 79–100.

Gardiner, D. and Nesbit, D. (1996) Cognitive Behavioural Groupwork with Male Offenders: The Newcastle upon Tyne Intensive Probation Unit, in Newburn, T. and Mair, G. *Working with Men*. Russell House Publishing.

Hamill, U. (1997) Practice Note: Merseyside Groupwork Programme for Men Who are Violent and Abusive to Their Partners. *Probation Journal*. 44: 2, Dec. 220–4.

Johnstone, M. (2000) Men, Masculity and Offending: Developing Gendered Practice in the Probation Service. *Probation Journal*. 48:1. March, 10–16.

Kemshall, H. and Pritchard, J. (1999) *Good Practice in Working with Violence*. Jessica Kingsley.

Lloyd, T. (1996) The Role of Training in the Development of Work with Men, in Newburn, T. and Mair, G. *Working with Men*. Russell House Publishing.

Morrison, D. (1997) Practice Note: Anger Control Work with Short Sentence and Remand Prisoners. *Probation Journal*. 44: 3, Sep. 157–9.

Murphy, K. (1996) Men and Offending Groups, in Newburn, T. and Mair, G. *Working with Men*. Russell House Publishing.

Newburn, T. and Mair, G. (1996) *Working with Men*. Russell House Publishing.

Stanton-Greenwood, A. (1999) Managing Violence in Residential Settings, in Kemshall, H. and Pritchard, J. (Eds.) (1999) *Good Practice in Working with Violence*. Jessica Kingsley.

Widom, C.S. (1989) The Cycle of Violence. *Science*. 244, 160–6.

CHAPTER 12

Mentoring socially excluded young people

Alison Skinner

Introduction

Mentoring in its original form is a very simple idea. An older experienced person befriends a younger man or woman, takes an interest in their progress, and provides advice and guidance in an informal manner. The name goes back to Homer's Greece, where it is recorded that Odysseus chose a mature older man called Mentor, to act as guardian and tutor to his son, while he was away from home.

Mentoring often happens in the workplace as a natural almost unconscious process, which the mentee might only see as significant in later life when looking back over their career. During the post war period, managers in the business field in America began to see the benefits of the mentoring process to their company in helping staff development and promoting equal opportunities, so employees were encouraged both to make use of mentors and act as one themselves. From being a largely middle class experience however, the notion has grown during the last 20 years, that disadvantaged and disaffected young people in trouble at school or in the community could also benefit from having an adult mentor to help them, drawn from outside their circle of friends and family.

A number of American schemes have been set up to recruit mentors and match them with young people. The best known is the organisation Big Brothers Big Sisters (BB/BS) which now matches 75,000 young people with mentors. An adult volunteer is paired with a young person from a single parent household. The volunteer agrees to meet the young person for about four hours, two to four times a month for at least a year. The relationship is supervised by a professional case manager. They undertake activities such as, going to a movie or play, school work, visiting the library, and sport.

A large scale evaluation of the BB/BS programme, carried out by Tierney, Grossman and Rech (1995) is still one of the best sources of evidence for mentoring effectiveness. A sample of young people matched with a mentor was compared with a similar number from the waiting list. The total number was 959 10–16 year olds. Most of the two groups came from low income households and a significant number came from households with a prior history of family violence or substance abuse. When the two groups were compared after 18 months it was found that participants in a BB/BS programme were:
- 46% less likely to start using drugs and alcohol
- 27% less likely to hit someone
- 52% less likely to miss a day at school

- 37% less likely to miss a class
- more likely to make modest gains in grade point average
- more likely to have improved peer and family relationships
- less likely to lie to parents or guardians

The organisation has now established itself in the UK and is running a version of its programme adapted to conditions in Britain.

Some mentoring projects try to make a difference for young people experiencing considerable disadvantage. Research evidence shows that considerable investment of time and resources is likely to be needed in these circumstances.

Royce (1998) studied the Brothers Project which was funded to prove that mentoring high-risk African American teenagers could have beneficial effects. The staff sought African American teenagers between the ages of 14 and 16, living in a female headed household who were underperforming in reading, maths and science. They were matched with African American volunteers who were usually college graduates.

A comparison was made between 36 young people who had received mentoring for six months or more, with a median length of 15 months, and 36 other young people with similar characteristics, who had not been mentored.

The study found that there was no statistically significant difference between the mentored group and the control group on self-esteem, attitudes to drugs and alcohol, school absences or disciplinary infractions. There was also no significant improvement in grade point average for the mentored group. The lack of difference still held good when the control group was compared with young people who had been mentored for 13 months or longer.

The authors suggest that longer matches of 24-30 months might be more beneficial, but also noted that many of the mentors did not report how long they spent with young people each month and no data was available about the quality of the relationship. They put forward a cautionary view of the degree of success that can be produced by a mentoring relationship with severely disadvantaged young people that rings true to British experience as well:

> Assuming that the typical mentor spent an average of two hours a week with his mentee, a 15 month relationship (which was the median) amounted to 120 hours of contact: and half the mentors were together with their mentees less time than that. Viewed from this perspective, the time together does not seem sufficient to offset poor school performance, negative influences on self-esteem and 14 or more years of living in poverty. While mentors can teach responsibility and values, discuss the importance of education and trying one's best and even provide a brief glimpse of some of the opportunities available in the larger world, they cannot be expected to completely neutralise the harsh conditions in which many of these adolescents live.
> (Royce, 1998)

This is an important perspective but it should not deter practitioners from trying mentoring as an approach with disadvantaged young people. Rather than seeing mentoring as a panacea for all young people's problems, a more pragmatic and realistic attitude would see mentoring as a useful methodology, which if properly organised and resourced, might well achieve valuable results with a range of young people. A cautious view would see its potential capacity to achieve really spectacular results with the most hardcore offenders as requiring sustained targeted intervention for at least a year and probably longer.

In Britain, mentoring has spread widely into many fields following the American example. It is common in industry and one of the most numerous approaches brings mentors from business into the classroom to provide role models for potentially underachieving students. In an era of league tables and national academic targets this is an attractive proposition for many head teachers, but using mentoring to work with students who are regularly absent from school or permanently excluded has been less common, although there are some school-based projects in cities such as Birmingham and Nottingham.

New Labour has embraced mentoring enthusiastically as a way of engaging with socially excluded young people in all kinds of settings and sponsored a number of new schemes, but there is a danger that the relationship could get devalued by overuse. The provision of 'earning mentors' in schools to help young people with their academic work has been agreed, as well as 'personal advisors' to assist with the transfer to vocational training and employment under the new *ConneXions* strategy. In addition, young people are allocated personal advisors during the Gateway Stage prior to New Traineeships at 16 and New Deal at 18 which can also be a mentor-type role.

Mentoring is now being advocated as a way of addressing the needs of young offenders following pioneering work by the Dalston Youth Project. Specific schemes sponsored by organisations which work with young people at risk such as Crime Concern, NACRO, RPS Rainer and SOVA have developed considerably during the past five years. The National Youth Justice Board has provided funding for local youth offending teams to develop mentoring schemes to work with young offenders at various stages in the tariff, especially final warning, published guidelines on how to run the schemes and commissioned an evaluation programme.

New projects need to be aware that between the ages of 14-18, their young people are potentially going to be in contact with a whole range of individuals authorised to develop a one-to-one mentoring type relationship with them to achieve various goals. This is in addition to any relationships with professional practitioners such as social workers, youth justice workers or detached youth workers, whom young people may have collected along the way, let alone possible links with the volunteers and befrienders described elsewhere in this book. This does not necessarily have to be a problem. It might be wise however for local authority and community-based projects, wanting to set up their own mentoring schemes, to conduct an audit of all the other people working with the young person in mentoring-type relationships and establish good lines of communication with them, to avoid duplication of effort and misunderstandings.

The following section sets out a range of issues which projects will need to think about in order to run successful mentoring schemes. This is based on the *Quality Framework for Mentoring with Socially Excluded Young People*, developed by the author and available from the National Mentoring Network.

What is mentoring?

A very wide range of activities is currently encompassed by the term 'mentoring' but there are a few core components:

- The relationship is likely to be time limited, although sometimes informal contacts may extend beyond this cut-off point unless forbidden by the project.
- It will usually be a one-to-one relationship although group mentoring happens in schools. Unless peer mentors are used, the mentor will usually be older than the young person. The degree to which they will be drawn from the same background and area will vary.
- The relationship will not be totally open-ended but used to achieve some agreed purpose:
  - to develop young people's skills
  - assist them to get launched in training or employment
  - develop new interests to avoid getting drawn into offending
  - improve relationships with their family and school if appropriate.

Mentors will advise, guide and support, and assist with the course of action agreed.

Mixed in with the formal aspects of the work will be the development of trust between the mentor and the young person, so that the latter feel confident enough to talk about important events happening in their life. Providing enough space for this to happen is an important part of the mentor's role, since young people in trouble often have complicated family relationships if they are living at home, or insecure and volatile lives if they are trying to survive independently. Mentoring programmes that start out being excessively task focused, usually find that young people are unable to concentrate on their official work programme until they have had a chance to talk about the personal matters uppermost in their minds. Providing a sympathetic ear and a certain amount of counselling support will be important skills needed by the mentor.

Setting up a mentoring programme

A project wanting to set up a mentoring scheme will need to consider how it will be funded. A budget will be needed for at least one full-time member of staff to co-ordinate the scheme and, depending on the numbers of young people, additional staff may also be desirable. Funding will be needed for recruitment, publicity, training of mentors and on-going volunteer expenses, over and above normal running costs.

Projects will need to decide on the type of young people they are targeting and what the mentors will be expected to achieve with them. They should then set out detailed referral criteria and circulate them to other agencies. These should be realistic; using a definition that is too broad, such as *supporting young people at risk*, may result in projects getting swamped. If young offenders are the target group, projects will need to be clear at what stage of the tariff they are intervening.

Ensuring that the mentoring relationship is a voluntary one, on the part of the young person, is a very important point of principle. For young offenders, unlike other young people, involvement in a mentoring programme may come with various strings attached, such as being a condition of a final warning or alternative to custody programme, with refusal having significant consequences for subsequent court appearances. If mentoring programmes for young offenders cannot be offered on a truly voluntary basis, this should be made clear from the start rather than fudging the issue. There may be some uncertainty about the nature of the relationship initially, on the part of young people, but this should be overcome eventually. Once the programme has its first young graduates, they will be able to assist in the recruitment of their peers.

Recruiting mentors

The key issues here are: what kind of mentor, and their age, sex and ethnic background.

What kind of mentors: adult or peer?

Although adult mentors are the most numerous, a number of projects have used peer mentors, to good effect. One advantage of this approach is that two young people instead of just one benefit from the programme, and it can enable a match to be made with young people of particular backgrounds which otherwise may be difficult. Young people who have been in residential care, for instance, will have had a particular range of experiences and adult mentors without that background, however well meaning, may struggle to achieve the degree of rapport in which real progress can be made.

Research by Skinner and Fleming (1999a) noted that adult mentors seemed to have two major motivations for getting involved with young people. One was the experience of having overcome similar problems in their youth and wanting to provide practical help to young people in difficulties. The other was a feeling of having had a more privileged background and wanting to put something back into the community. In the latter case it may be necessary to be clear what such a person is bringing to the mentoring relationship, to ensure that the benefits of the relationship are not all one way.

Age, sex and ethnic background

A number of young people expressed a wish for mentors who were not too much older than themselves. This should be heeded, although it might be difficult to achieve. An examination of the gender ratio in mentoring projects revealed that in community-based projects more women are likely to be recruited than men and few males from minority ethnic groups come forward as mentors from routine recruitment. Special effort on the part of the project will be needed to overcome this natural bias. Unsurprisingly, mentoring projects catering exclusively for black young people were most successful in recruiting black staff. One resourceful project of this kind noted, 'We do a lot of word of mouth, but we do advertise as well in strange ways. We ask schools to find us mentors, we ask anyone. We advertise in the barbers' shops, we ask some of the men there. We do workshops with a whole range of churches.'

Spreading the net widely and using a range of methods to recruit mentors is likely to have better results than relying exclusively on word of mouth, particularly if the network activated consists of people with very similar characteristics and background.

Training mentors

The degree of training and support received by mentors is often crucial in determining how successfully they manage to work with young people. Within the mentoring field there is an enormous variation in the amount of training provided for mentors, ranging from one hour to several days. Organisations such as Crime Concern, SOVA and RPS Rainer provide very well resourced and focused training for their mentors working with young offenders. As a minimum, mentors will have to be fully briefed about the Criminal Justice system as well as sensitised to factors in the young person's background and experience that are likely to be influential. The bigger the social gap between mentors and the young people they are matched with, the more important this initial training is likely to be.

Training provided at a more substantive level will provide guidance on a whole range of boundary issues, including confidentiality and health and safety issues and offer the chance to listen to case studies and scenarios. Once they have been trained and matched, some projects organise peer group meetings for their mentors so they can draw support from each other and compare notes. These are always well received.

Matching young people and mentors

It is uncommon in the mentoring field for young people to meet their mentor before they are matched with them, but this is highly desirable as part of the process. In most cases it is the project co-ordinator who meets and gathers information from both sides and makes the link. Young people are usually allowed to reject a match but have little opportunity to exercise a positive choice. Asking young people to specify desirable characteristics they would like in their mentor is good practice, but being able to respond positively to these requests is important. A number of projects working with young people at risk and young offenders run residentials which allow both sides to have a sight of each other before committing themselves. While this is not foolproof, it does seem to help with the bonding process.

Issues around matching gender and ethnic background will often exercise project co-ordinators. Projects working with young offenders will usually have more males than females and because it is harder to recruit male mentors than females ones, particularly for community-based projects, many young male offenders will end up being mentored by women. This can work well and sometimes young men feel more comfortable talking about personal matters to women rather than men. However, it does not address the need to find positive male role models for these young people, who may have most of their significant relationships at home and at school with women.

On ethnic background, the findings from our research showed that white mentors believed that they could mentor young people from a range of ethnic groups quite effectively. In contrast, minority ethnic young people, particularly from the Asian community, were clear in their desire for a mentor from the same cultural background, even if they belonged to a different faith group.

Working with young people

Mentors and young people will agree action plans at the start of their programme. These will have some broad objectives but should be flexible enough to adapt to changing circumstances. Mentoring programmes for young offenders are usually longer than other kinds, lasting for six to twelve months. Weekly meetings of at least two hours duration are generally the norm for this type of project and mentors and young people will usually meet in the community to do various activities.

There is keen debate in the field about the issue of payment of mentors. Mentors who are in work will usually see this activity as voluntary, but potential mentors who are unemployed may need alternative arrangements. Having flexible policies catering to the individual circumstances of mentors is likely to have the best effect. Projects should pay travel and out-of-pocket expenses arising from the meetings with young people. Parents or carers should not be expected to subsidise projects of this kind. Paying childcare expenses to enable female mentors to participate fully in any social or training opportunities will also need to be considered.

If meetings are to be unsupervised, clear boundaries and safety procedures must be in place to safeguard both sides, communicated in training and fully understood by both young people and mentors. As a matter of good practice, all mentors should be police vetted before undertaking this work.

Mentoring schemes vary according to the degree to which young people can contact their mentor outside the specified hours. Female mentors and young women often bond very quickly and there appears to be a greater willingness on the part of adult women in these matches to provide home telephone numbers and out-of-hours support. One committed female mentor talked her young person down after a spectacular family row and a middle-of-the-night departure from home. Such trust is not always extended to young male offenders who appear to be more often subject to project rules and restrictions regarding contact. In projects involving young offenders, out-of-hours contact is usually made via the project.

Mentors have to be prepared through their training for set-backs in the relationship, when young people seem not to be making any progress at all, or are too overwhelmed with personal problems to address their action plan requirements. Mentors from one project working with homeless young people were particularly attuned to this problem:

> . . . problem of keeping the mentoring moving, so much slower than I thought it would be.
> . . . Feeling really frustrated. I want to get going and sort the person's life out, but the young people aren't able to move so fast.

Regular supervision and support for the mentor from the project co-ordinator will be extremely important in these circumstances. Good practice in this instance could include regular phone contact by the project worker responsible, additional training, mentor group meetings and a one-to-one mentor 'buddy' system.

Projects have also recognised that young people need support during the mentoring relationship, which is usually supplied by a key member of staff meeting regularly with them. Projects working with young offenders often organise group meetings as well, in one case paying the young people £5 to turn up.

Mentoring projects are also very demanding on project co-ordinators and some form of formal or informal professional support should also be provided for them.

Projects should be aware of the need to prepare young people for the end of the mentoring relationship, which will become more significant to both sides the longer it goes on. Most projects working with young offenders have a fixed ending and mentors will be advised not to continue the link beyond that apart from the exchange of birthday or Christmas cards. Projects working with other groups may be a little more flexible.

At the end of the relationship, action plans will be reviewed, and projects should take the opportunity of getting detailed feedback from both mentors and young people in order to improve their practice. This should include assessment of how the project performed in support, as well as the outcomes of the mentoring relationship. The degree of success of the mentoring programme will depend on the targets set for it and outcomes are usually evaluated at the point of maximum impact at the end of the programme. Along with other types of supervised activities, a mentoring programme should be able to reduce the incidence of offending while it is in progress and many will assist young people to get into work or training programmes. Outcomes at six to twelve months later, however, may be a more realistic assessment of long-term effects.

As graduates of the mentoring programme, young people may be eligible to train as peer mentors or otherwise provide support to the project. Their experience is an important asset that could be used at conferences and training events of many kinds.

Quality framework

Many of the issues discussed earlier feature as key points in the *Quality Framework for Mentoring with Socially Excluded Young People* created by the author on behalf of the National Mentoring Network. This document, in full or summary form, is available free of charge from this organisation, along with the research report *Mentoring Socially Excluded Young People*. These reports will provide detailed guidance for projects interested in setting up mentoring schemes.

Conclusions

At its best, mentoring is an extremely powerful form of practice that can give young people a quality of personal help and support rarely matched by other methods. The key determinate however is the degree of planning, training and support available to the mentor and young people which will need to be considerable, to achieve the best and most long lasting effects. Young people who do not know what the relationship is supposed to achieve, and mentors who do not know what the boundaries are, will not achieve significant results, even if they have been matched and set up to meet weekly for six months.

The National Mentoring Network can provide links with other projects and the national organisations, NACRO, Crime Concern, SOVA and RPS Rainer are a valuable source of information on mentoring practice with young offenders and young people at risk.

References

Royce, D. (1998) Mentoring High Risk Minority Youth: Evaluation of the Brothers Project. *Adolescence.* 33: 129, 145–58.

Skinner, A. and Fleming, J. (1999a) *Mentoring Socially Excluded Young People: Lessons from Practice.* The National Mentoring Network.

Skinner, A. and Fleming, J. (1999b) *Quality Framework for Mentoring with Socially Excluded Young People.* The National Mentoring Network.

Tierney, J. et al. (1995) *Making a Difference: An Impact Study of Big Brother/Big Sister.* Public/Private Ventures.

Copies of the *Quality Framework* and *Mentoring Socially Excluded Young People* are available from National Mentoring Network, First Floor, Charles House, Albert St, Eccles, Manchester M30 0PD.

CHAPTER 13

Participative evaluation

Jennie Fleming

Introduction

Readers of this chapter may have had a variety of experiences of evaluation. Workers in youth justice projects will be used to statistical types of evaluation that seek to measure the impact of their programmes on young people's offending behaviour. They may be less familiar, however, with approaches which seek to enable young people to influence the scope and direction of the evaluation and maybe even take an active role in the collection and analysis of the information.

Some workers in community based and voluntary projects, particularly those which are newly set up, may be aware of the need to evaluate but are less certain of where to start and what might be useful types of information to collect.

This chapter considers the purposes of evaluation, the advantages of meaningfully involving young people, and possible methods of collecting information, and sets out an overall process that can be adapted to different projects and situations.

What is evaluation?

There is an important distinction between monitoring and evaluation. **Monitoring** is checking out if things are happening according to the plan you set out. **Evaluation** is about seeing how effective and efficient you have been in reaching your goals.

It is important to know if something has been successful, or not. Sometimes this is because the funders or sponsors want to know how things have gone, but also importantly because workers themselves want to know if what they set out to do has worked or not, and what works best. If you want to share the successes of your community based youth justice project, or show that resources are being well used, or highlight gaps in the service you provide, then evaluation can help you do this.

Evaluation helps you to know whether you have been effective or not. It is a crucial part of practice development. What information is collected and how, will depend on what you are trying to do and how you think it can be shown and shared. Outcome evaluation is concerned with assessing *what* an activity has achieved. Process evaluation tries to explain *how* it has been brought about (Aggleton et al., 1992). All these aspects of evaluation can build up a picture of a particular activity, relationship or project.

Why evaluate?

In the twenty-first century it is quite accepted that evaluation is a fundamental part of much work with young people, though perhaps there are still anxieties about how best to do it and at times how it will be used and interpreted. However, there are often a number of different rationales for undertaking an evaluation. Feuerstein (1986) records a number of different answers given to the question, 'why did you evaluate?'.

- Achievement (seeing what has been achieved).
- Measuring progress (in accordance with the aims and objectives of the programme).
- Improving monitoring (for better management).
- Identifying strengths and weaknesses (to strengthen the programme).
- Seeing if the effort was effective (what difference has the programme made?).
- Cost benefit (were the costs reasonable?).
- Collecting information (to plan and manage programme activities better).
- Sharing experiences (to prevent others making similar mistakes, or to encourage them to use similar methods).
- Improving effectiveness (to have more impact).
- Allowing for better planning (more in line with the needs of people, especially at community level).

It is possible to devise an evaluation process for projects that addresses all these elements.

The value base of evaluation

Evaluation does not take place in a vacuum. Youth justice and voluntary projects might be subject to scrutiny by many different interest groups: the police, the courts, schools, parents, volunteers, residents' groups and politicians to name a few. These groups will have their own interpretation of the findings of any evaluation. Youth crime is seen as an important issue and a range of values and beliefs will be reflected in the responses to your evaluation. If the purpose of youth justice work is seen solely (or principally) in terms of crime reduction then figures on criminal activity could be recorded. However, if the purpose of your project includes objectives like:

> . . . to provide a positive role model and means of practical support to those young people involved in the youth justice system, to help them tackle the issues in their lives, which put them at risk of further offending . . .
>
> (from a leaflet produced by The Interventions Team Mentoring Project, Leicester, Leicestershire and Rutland)

then wider questions must be asked to establish if this is happening.

It is important that if your project is committed to the empowerment and education of young people then your evaluation methods need to reflect this too. All social activity has an impact and effect; evaluation is not a neutral activity but like practice, is affected by values. An evaluation of services can cover a range of measures, taking in tick box questionnaires, defined by professionals at one end, or focus groups of users who identify what the issues are for them at the other. Similar starting points but different ways of working, because of different values and ways of seeing the world. In all social intervention you need to be clear about your value position before you start and evaluation is a form of social intervention.

Involving young people in the evaluation

It is important to consider how to involve the young people who use your project in any evaluation. There is a continuum of possibilities for this. At one end you could just expect them to fill in the questionnaires that you have designed, at the other they could have been involved in the whole process of evaluation. This would mean they would be involved in deciding what to investigate, how to collect the information and who to ask. Being researchers or information gatherers themselves, they would also play a part in the analysis and presentation of the findings. The Joseph Rowntree Foundation and Save the Children have produced a number of excellent, very practical books on the involvement of children and young people in participatory research and evaluation; see for example Kirby (1999), Worrall (2000) and Ward (1997a). These are good practical guides and I suggest anyone interested in involving young people in the evaluation of their project, reads them.

As Kirby writes:

> *Participatory research is not just about improved research methods. It is also about achieving democratic participation and social justice for children and young people. By influencing what is researched, and how their lives are represented, they participate in institutional decision-making processes. The more young people become actively engaged in research, the more they personally gain, and the more they may expect, and demand, that changes come out of the findings.* (Kirby, 1999)

The Centre for Social Action (see Chapter 1) would strongly recommend that you look to maximise the involvement of young people in the evaluation of the work of your youth justice project. You should look for ways to build this in from the very beginning: talking with them about evaluation and what it means, to the very end when 'findings' are analysed and presented. Exactly how far you can do this and what it will look like will depend on your project. There is no doubt that projects which already have group work or forums for discussion will find it easier, but all projects will benefit from considering how they can involve young people in the evaluation.

When to evaluate?

Ideally, evaluation should be planned alongside the development of the project or activity and it should not be tacked on at the end. It should take place throughout the life of the project. As the goals, aims and objectives are being established, so there should be discussion alongside this of how project workers will know they have been achieved. Having said that, it is never too late to start and a carefully planned evaluation at the end of a project is better than nothing.

At this point is also important to mention that a whole project evaluation, which may be a snapshot at one particular time, can build on the on-going evaluation of parts of the project. So you could evaluate all your training days, courses, trips, series of activity sessions, have reviews of work on a regular basis and this information would be compiled and form part of a whole project evaluation.

How you are going to use your evaluation will also determine when it is set up. Do your funders need the information to be able to make decisions? Are young people leaving your project at a particular time? Check out that you are not missing important opportunities by your timing.

Types of information that could be collected

It is quite possible to get carried away with information collection; the availability of computers means that it can easily be stored. You do not want to over burden people, or yourself, with too many questions. It is the Centre's experience that projects working in the youth justice field are prepared to ask more intrusive questions of young people than would be tolerated in youth work generally. Also, it has sometimes happened that their service-users are used as a source of information about the profile of young offenders in the area and they are asked for information that is not necessary for the evaluation of the project. So think carefully about what you collect: is it necessary? Is it useful? What does it show about your work?

Undoubtedly you will need to collect a certain amount of quantitative data. You will need to know how many young people use your project, who refers them or how they found out about it. You will need to know how many are male and female and what ethnic groups they are from to ensure your service is truly accessible to all it should be. There may be other things that are required by the parameters of your project. It is important that you establish very early on, easy and useable systems for collecting this type of monitoring information and that you have the means for pulling out the information you need.

As Bailey and Williams report, some practitioners in youth offending teams are concerned about the tendency to rely on names and statistics, which sometimes misses the broader picture:

> *A worker described working with a young person who had stopped using drugs and started attending school during a period of supervision, but had also re-offended. While this is likely to be seen as a failure from a statistical point of view, the intervention might be seen as successful overall.*   (Bailey and Williams, 2001)

Alongside these figures you will also need to collect qualitative information. This is where you will get the richness and depth, 'providing vivid descriptions and clear insights into problems and opportunities' (Ward, 1997a). For this, open-ended questions are a good method: questions which explore how people think things have happened, or not, and why some things have worked, or not. Written questionnaires, where the questions are pre-set and even the answers are decided in advance, so all respondents do is choose from a pre-determined list of options, are not, in our experience, a good way of getting in-depth information and understanding of what involvement in a project has meant to a young person.

It is likely you will select a variety of indicators to evaluate your project. One final word of caution; care is needed in describing the relationship between cause and effect. Young people have busy lives with many influences, both positive and negative on them, and your work is just one small part. Changes in young people's attitudes and behaviours might be due to many things, of which your intervention is but one. Be careful not to attribute too much to the effect of the project's work. The relationship between your work and changes in the young people can be inferred but not proven (Voluntary Activity Unit, 1997b).

Evaluation is not only about how well objectives have been met. There will also be unintended consequences of what you have done and these need to be included too. Once again broad brush, open-ended forms of inquiry will aid this. For example, 'What has your involvement in the project meant to you?' will elicit all kinds of responses you might not have foreseen.

Finally, it is important not to expect too much of evaluation. You need to be realistic about what can be done within the time and resources available. Not all your questions will be answered, so it is important to think through carefully and agree what key questions the evaluation needs to address.

Possible methods of collecting information

There are many text books on research and evaluation, some of which simply explain techniques that you can use in your evaluation, see for example Denscombe (1998), Feuerstein (1986), Aggleton et al. (1992), Mikkelsen (1995). The last three emphasize participatory methods. Whilst none of these are written specifically about the evaluation of youth justice projects however, they are easily adaptable to many work situations.

You need to decide the most appropriate methods to evaluate your particular project. There is no 'right way' to approach information collection. You need to get information by a variety of means. Exactly how you collect information will be decided hopefully in discussion with young people, and your evaluation steering group or management committee if you have one.

One important aspect is getting the views of all the people who have been involved in your project or activity, such as practitioners, volunteers and referrers. This process can be done in many ways. These include:

- direct observation
- guided conversations with key individuals and groups
- critical incident analysis e.g. resource and facility maps
- drama workshops
- case studies of organisations and individuals
- work diaries of paid and unpaid workers and young people
- focus groups
- SWOT analysis (looking at the strengths, weaknesses, opportunities and threats in particular situations)
- questionnaires
- statistical data   (Fleming and Ward, 1999; Mikkelsen, 1995)

The Voluntary Activity Unit (1997b) point out that these can be condensed into 'to observe, to ask questions, to consult existing records'. Within 'to ask questions' particularly, there are many ways to do this. Many of the activities described by Skinner in Chapter 1 and the stages of the social action process, can readily be adapted to evaluation.

A process to develop a participative evaluation approach

This process can be adapted and applied by community based youth justice projects to both single activities, for example a residential or a group, to look at offending behaviour, or to a large-scale evaluation of a whole project.

The first stage as discussed earlier, is to establish clear goals, aims and objectives, for the project or activity. By setting well-defined aims and objectives that identify what you are hoping to achieve it is easier to know what to evaluate. The success of any activity may be measured by the extent to which these objectives are reached. Whilst those set out in funding applications will play a role in your evaluation, it is important to also talk with staff, funders, volunteers, service users and others with an interest, maybe parents, local residents, victims of crime as well, about their hopes and fears for the project and their involvement with it.

A case study

The Centre for Social Action believes it is the role of an evaluator to facilitate a process which encourages people to set their own agendas and which includes self-assessment and participation by all parts of the project. This process conducted by Jennie Fleming using social action principles is illustrated by a case study of the evaluation of a project working with young homeless people.

The agreed approach in this case was that the worker from the Centre would collaborate with the project to develop methods of evaluation which would cover all aspects of their work, allowing for them to be used both internally and externally. The Centre would produce an evaluation report after two years for external use, but the systems developed would continue to be used by project staff and users for the life of the project.

The evaluator suggested the creation of a monitoring and evaluation sub-group to include workers, volunteers, managers, board members and an external evaluator. They would be responsible for making decisions about what information was collected, how it was best done and also the interpretation, discussion and dissemination of information.

The starting point for developing the evaluation strategy was for the worker to talk to funders and board members about the kind of information they would like to receive about the project. She also had a session with the practitioner team to look at the shared values that underpinned their work, how they put these values into practice and how they might know they were being successful. There were also discussions about what information they would find useful and also how such information could be collected. She also had sessions with young people as users of the services to find out what it was they wanted from the project. Young people were also asked how they thought it would be best to collect the views and opinions of young people. All this information was used to help shape the evaluation tools and methods, in ways that would encourage the participation of all involved.

The project needed to be able to monitor the day-to-day use of its building based services, and information about contact between young people and workers. Reflecting this requirement and drawing on the earlier discussions, the evaluator constructed some simple data collection forms that enabled the workers to record factual information and young people to supply self-assessed equal opportunity information.

Collecting information about the views of young people, social workers and people from other agencies, on the quality of the service they received, what they most appreciated about the project and any complaints or recommendations for change they wanted to make, was not quite so straightforward. For this, a variety of methods were used. Central to the evaluation of a project like this, committed to user involvement, was process evaluation and representation of users' views. The young people had suggested a comments board where people could write ideas and thoughts; a more private 'suggestions box' was created as well. Simple and straightforward questions for the evaluation of specific events and activities, groupwork, parenting skills courses, social evenings, were devised with the steering group and piloted. Workers ensured they were used and looked for ways to build evaluation into the project's activities and ways of working, rather than just tacking it on the outside.

All the information from the initial discussions was compiled and used to produce interview schedules for conversations with all the groups of people involved in the project.

It was felt to be important that, as far as possible, all the different groups of people involved with the project were asked basically the same questions. This enabled different perspectives on the same issues to be collected. The questions put the emphasis on exploring expectations *and* feelings during initial contact with the project, and checking that at all stages of young people's involvement with it, they felt they were listened to, supported and given the opportunity to say what was uppermost in their minds.

There were group discussions with the young people to obtain their views and project workers were very helpful in providing them with lifts, in order to ensure they were able to attend these meetings. These were settings where the young people felt comfortable and seemed able to speak freely. Young people also had individual interviews and some were interviewed on the telephone. This was a suggestion from the young people themselves and one the evaluator was not totally convinced by, until it was tried out and found to work very well indeed, with the young people talking freely about what they thought of the project.

The project workers contributed to the evaluation through a meeting with the evaluator, where they brainstormed their perceptions of the impact of the project under the headings of:
- Achievements.
- Last year's aims: how have we done?
- Factors that help and hinder our work.
- Hopes for the next 12 months.

Social workers, workers from other agencies and some parents contributed to the evaluation by group discussions (social services team meetings), individual and telephone interviews. Some social workers chose to write their views down, so a written questionnaire was produced.

This participative evaluation made a significant difference to the way in which the agency organised its services. They changed their opening hours and added to their range of services. They also set up a young people's committee that eventually had representation on the Board.

Stages of evaluation

A participatory evaluation could include the following stages, all undertaken with young people:
1. Agree who the evaluation is for.
2. Agree who will make decisions about the evaluation.
3. Decide on the resources needed.
4. Establish the parameters of the evaluation (taking into account all the various interests and expectations).
5. Agree how you will 'measure' what has happened.
6. Decide how the information will be collected.
7. Agree who will collect the information.
8. Collect the information in a variety of ways (this can be an on-going process).

9. Think about what the information shows and tells you about the project.
10. Tell people about the results.
11. Take action in line with the findings of your evaluation.
12. Evaluate the evaluation.   (loosely adapted from Voluntary Activity Unit, 1997b)

Agree who the evaluation is for

Different groups will have different expectations of the evaluation. For example, funders and workers might well have different interests in the evaluation. As far as possible, the evaluation should try and meet everyone's needs in one exercise. If this is not possible, you should be clear about this from the start and possibly negotiate with different interest groups to alter their expectations.

Agree who will make decisions about the evaluation

Are you going to have an evaluation group? Who will be on it? What role will young people play in the evaluation? Will this include all young people or a group? Do all people have an equal say?

Decide on the resources needed

Evaluation takes time and participative evaluation can take even longer. If you are going to take a collaborative and participative approach to your evaluation you will need to allow time for people to get together and talk. Time is the major resource needed in participative evaluation, whether it is ensuring you allow time at the end of a day event for people to make their comments, or in co-ordinating a series of special meetings to collect people's views of the project.

As is pointed out in *Measuring Community Development in Northern Ireland*:

> Easily available information is not necessarily the most useful: it is easier to count heads than ask whether people are satisfied.   (Voluntary Activity Unit, 1997b)

There are costs and benefits surrounding evaluation and each project has to keep the balance between these.

Establish the parameters of the evaluation

Social action evaluation works on the basis that evaluation should not be distanced from the practical work of the project. All people with an interest should be involved in the discussions and decisions about what is to be evaluated. It is not a time to specify fixed questions as there is a real need to be flexible and to allow people to raise the issues they think are important. It may just be necessary to ask people at the beginning of a session what they hope to have achieved by the end, and follow-up by making sure you do ask at the end whether this has happened. If it is a whole project evaluation you are planning, it might be important to think of the community and environment of which the project is a part. You may want to include their views in the evaluation.

Agree how you will 'measure' what has happened

These 'measurements' will be affected by the work you are doing and how much money and resources you have available. To carry out an evaluation you need to agree on a way of knowing whether something has happened. You may want to find out about measures that have been used by similar projects, or borrow ideas from a participative qualitative evaluation in any community based project. However, some possible measures include:

- Young people's views on their relationships with workers, family members or volunteers.
- Changes in behaviour.
- Changes in attitude.
- Levels of self confidence.
- How much young people enjoy coming to the project or session.
- Whether people have used new knowledge or skills.
- Changes in policy.
- Changes in the delivery of other services for young people.

Just knowing what has happened is not enough, it is crucial to know *why* people think things have happened, as this is important information for project development or to help people, yourselves or others, repeat your successes. Ensure you find ways to explore this in your evaluation.

Decide how the information will be collected

Be imaginative! Yes, talking is important, but think of other ways too. Photos, videos, graffiti walls, video or audiotape boxes, drama, drawings, posters, stories. Just be sure to leave the interpretation of these things to the people who have produced them.

Inevitably some of your evaluation will be based on words. Care is needed with how any questions or prompts are worded. On a recent evaluation we undertook of a community-based project for young homeless people, we talked with the young people in groups, and individually, with such prompts for discussion as:

> *How do you decide what you do and talk about with your key worker?*
> *In what ways does the project give you the support that you need?*
> *How would you describe the project to another young person?*
> *What would you like to see changed in the project?*

Remember those '*why?*' questions too.

Agree who will collect the information

There are issues of objectivity and resources to be considered in making this decision. Young people could be trained and supported to collect the information, and an outside agency could be employed to ensure impartiality. The time it will take needs to be given careful consideration.

Collect the information

Evaluation is not a one-off thing, it should be integral to your work and an on-going process. This can mean checking throughout your training session that people are happy and learning what they need to, as well as a more formal evaluation at the end. It also means ensuring you are finding out what young people think of the project on an on-going basis as well as undertaking an annual review of your work including all parties.

Think about what the information shows and tells you about the project

Whatever involvement young people and other interested parties have had up until now, it is important that they are included in these discussions. You will need to both analyse and interpret the information. *Analysing the information*, means looking at it and seeing if there are any patterns or themes. *Interpreting the information* means identifying the implications and importance of what you have found out.

Tell people about the findings

Everybody who is involved should be given some information about the findings. It is usual to produce some kind of written report as a summary of the findings, their analysis and interpretation. It is also important that you describe how the information is collected so that readers can make their own assessment of its validity. It is worth thinking about *why* the evaluation was undertaken and *who* the evaluation is for. It is also important to think about *when* the findings are needed. Your evaluation might be written or might use multi-media or both. You might produce displays, videos, presentations, a meeting where people can hear about and discuss the findings, or a newsletter for all concerned. Think about the ways that the people you want to talk to about the findings, are going to find the most accessible. You may also want to share your evaluation through any professional or community networks, and with other voluntary or youth justice projects.

Take action in line with the findings

The key purpose of the evaluation is to ensure you are doing a good job. It is important that as information emerges about your project you act on it and incorporate it into your practice. If changes are needed, be prepared to make them. Learn from your strengths and see how more can be made of them.

However, your evaluation might produce information that can be used in other ways too. For example, campaigning on young people's rights, influencing the practice of others, developing new services or influencing policy. In our evaluations of non-governmental organisations' work with young people, the young people often compare workers in these projects very favourably to social workers and make criticisms of the way social services operate. The Centre for Social Action has looked for ways of sharing this information with social services, both specifically and generally.

Evaluate the evaluation

Has it worked? Did you ask the right questions, the right people, in the right ways? How could you do it better another time? Start the preparations for the next cycle of evaluation.

Conclusions

Evaluation is fundamentally about judging the worth of an activity, but despite this, evaluation can sometimes be viewed as a chore, a public relations exercise, or a source of considerable anxiety. It does not have to be any of these things. Evaluation does not need to be difficult or intimidating, but it does need thought and planning (Coppel, 1999). Many of the approaches discussed in this chapter could allow considerable creativity in the way that the evaluation is tackled, even creating the possibility that evaluation can not only be useful, but fun. By opening up the planning and practice to many other people, the responsibility can be shared out and not rest exclusively with the project leader. Engaging fully with young people in the ways suggested may lead to greater insights into aspects of your practice that appear to make a difference. This is valuable information to share widely, both inside and outside your team.

References

Aggleton, P., Moody, D. and Young, A. (1992) *Evaluating HIV/AIDS Health Promotion: A Resource for HIV/AIDS Health Promotion Workers in Statutory and Voluntary Organisations.* Health Education Authority.

Bailey, R. and Williams, B. (2001) No Soft Option. *Community Care.* 11–17 Jan. 24–5.

Coppel, D. (1999) *An Evaluation Resource Pack for HAZ Projects.* Nottingham Health Action Zone.

Denscombe, M. (1998) *The Good Research Guide for Small-scale Social Research Project.* Open University Press.

Feuerstein, M. (1986) *Partners in Evaluation: Evaluating Development and Community Programmes with Participants.* Macmillan.

Fleming, J. and Ward, W. (1999) Research as Empowerment: The Social Action Approach, in Shera, W. and Wells, L. (Eds.) *Empowerment Practice in Social Work.* Canadian Scholars' Press.

Kirby, P. (1999) *Involving Young Researchers: How to Enable Young People to Design and Conduct Research.* Joseph Rowntree Foundation.

Mikkelsen, B. (1995) *Methods for Development Work and Research: A Guide for Practitioners.* Sage.

Skinner, A. and Harrison, M. Community and Neighbourhood Strategies in Work with Young People at Risk.

Voluntary Activity Unit (1997a) *Monitoring and Evaluation of Community Development in Northern Ireland.* Dept of Health and Social Services.

Voluntary Activity Unit (1997b) *Measuring Community Development in Northern Ireland; A Handbook for Practitioners.* Dept of Health and Social Services.

Ward, D. (1997a) Social Action Research: A Methodology for Addressing 'How it is'. *Social Action Journal.* 3: 229–32.

Ward, L. (1997b) *Seen and Heard: Involving Disabled Children and Young People in Research and Development Projects.* Joseph Rowntree Foundation.

Worrall, S. (2000) *Young People as Researchers: A Learning Resource Pack.* Save the Children.

Conclusions

Alan Dearling and Alison Skinner

Probably it is a truism in a book such as this to say that there are no conclusions, only challenges, and possibilities.

Working with young people, especially those who are troubled or troublesome, is never about easy options. Roger Graef, the prominent documentary film maker summed it up succinctly:

> There is a kind of hole in our thinking about these young people that I see needs filling by people who are willing to engage, who are willing to put up with being stood up four times in a row, who are willing to be disappointed but to stay with it and treat these young people in the same way we would treat our own children. (Graef, 2000)

We believe that this sort of inclusive approach lies at the heart of any work with young people, whether they have offended or not. Young people deserve respect, support, empathy and care as well as guidance, counselling or elements of control. In the media young people are frequently only portrayed as perpetrators of crime, but in reality many face:

- violence in the home and on the streets
- victimisation
- poor housing, health, education and social conditions
- lack of employment possibilities

Throughout this book we have tried to present practice examples and strategies for working which help to offer young people alternatives to offending behaviour. In this first decade of the new millennium, community safety and crime prevention initiatives need to continue to prioritise initiatives that are:

- child-centred
- enabling and empowering
- holistic
- fair
- appropriate

In 1999, Home Office Minister of State, Charles Clarke stressed the need for youth crime prevention initiatives which actively encouraged personal development. He said:

> Working to divert young people should not be seen simply as following a criminal justice agenda: youth work can help young people in important ways to fulfil their potential as individuals and prepare them for active citizenship with a real stake in society's wellbeing.

Peter Loewenstein (1999) suggested that youth work needed to be 'harnessed in youth offending teams and crime reduction partnerships' to achieve these ends. We still strongly believe that, and